The Miracle of Faith

(Five Homilies)

Archimandrite Daniel Gouvalis

Translated by
Fr. Nicholas Palis and Lawrence Damian Robinson

Edited and Annotated by
Lawrence Damian Robinson

Ἐπίγνωσις

EPIGNOSIS PUBLISHING

The Miracle of Faith

Copyright © 2014 by Lawrence Damian Robinson and Nicholas Palis

Epignosis Publishing
P.O. Box 682
Princeton, NJ 08542-0682

The Epignosis Publishing name and logo are trademarks of Epignosis Publishing in the United States of America. For rights inquiries, contact: publisher@epignosispublishing.com.

First edition: August 2014
20 19 18 17 16 15 14 13 12 11   1 2 3 4 5
ISBN: 978-0-6922520-5-5

Library of Congress Control Number: 2014912443

The Miracle of Faith

Discussion at a Monastery by Monk Macarius

"Whatever God creates, man cannot destroy."

—General I. Makrygiannis[1]

(*Visions and Miracles*, 83)

---

[1] Ioannis Makrygiannis (1797-1864) was one of the heroes of the Greek War of Independence against the Ottoman Empire, and one of the early Greek state's most notable politicians and writers.—*Ed.*

The Very Reverend Archimandrite Daniel Gouvalis
of Blessed Memory (1940-2009†).

Contents

List of Photographs

LIST OF PHOTOGRAPHS (CONT'D)

Translators' Foreword

We live in a time in which it seems that our faith is under constant assault from all sides, both overtly and covertly, directly and indirectly. Whether it is due to the unceasing bombardment by explicit images and subliminal messages telling us to value the fleeting pleasures of the passions and of the flesh above all else, or the invisible consequences of the increasing complexity of a daily life that seeks to "choke the word" in us with "the cares of this world and the deceitfulness of riches" (Mt. 13:22), we are all too often made to feel small, inadequate, isolated, and insignificant.

In short, we are made to feel helpless and hopeless; and in losing hope, we run the grave risk to our souls of also losing our faith. Indeed, it is not without reason that our Lord and Savior Jesus Christ asks: "When the Son of Man comes, will he find the faith on earth?" (Lk 18:8)

Fortunately for us, when we cry out from the

depths of our heart like the man whose son was possessed—"I believe, O Lord, help my unbelief!"—we see that God's mercy is quick to find us. And undoubtedly a very big part of that mercy is the fact that throughout every age, the Church has been graced with the presence of holy elders and saints who have—through their words and the example of their lives—helped to strengthen and increase the faith of God's people.

One such elder, though little known in the West, was the very reverend Archimandrite Daniel Gouvalis of blessed memory. Born in 1940 in the little village of Panourgias, in the foothills of the imposing Mt. Gionas, Fr. Daniel spent his childhood in the difficult and dangerous environment of first the Nazi Occupation and then the Greek Civil War.

As a young man, Fr. Daniel was sent to live with relatives in Piraeus (Athens), where he attended high school. While there, he occupied a corner of his uncle's small, unheated dairy shop and slept on a plain wood-plank cot, without even a mattress. It was during this time in Piraeus that he met his first spiritual father, Fr. Cherubim—an Athonite priest-monk and founder of the Holy Monastery of the Paraclete outside of Oropos, Attica—who took a compassionate interest in the sensitive and earnest young man.

When Fr. Daniel finished his studies at the Theological School of the National Capodistrian University of Athens, and completed his military service, he was tonsured as a monk by Fr. Cherubim and ordained to the deaconate and the priesthood. After Fr. Cherubim's repose, Fr. Daniel became a spiritual child of the recently glorified St. Porphyrios, with whom he maintained a close personal relationship for many years.

For twenty-five years, Fr. Daniel served as the priest of the small parish of St. Paraskevi in Malakasa, near the town of Oropos. He was extremely active there in serving the needs of his congregation and of his numerous spiritual children, as well as in his writing and his work in defense of the Orthodox faithful against the influence of modern religious sects. In regard to the latter, he was a longtime member of the 'Special Synodical Committee for the Study of Ancient Cults and New Paganism' of the Church of Greece.

While a detailed biography of Fr. Daniel is beyond the scope of this foreword, there were a few personal characteristics of this extraordinary holy man and grace-filled priest that not only stood out as noteworthy, but which demand mention. Among them were his gentle, unassuming, and unimposing manner; his quiet joyfulness, childlike simplicity, the constant warm twinkle in his eye, and his unexpected and occasionally even mischievous (in a good-natured way) sense of humor; his love for his fellow man, and especially for children, and for all of creation and the natural world.

There were also his selfless and tireless efforts and activities in service to the Church and to his spiritual children: frequent, long hours of holy confession; visits to the sick and the suffering in every part of Greece; liturgies, supplications services and vigils; trips and excursions with his spiritual children to pilgrimage sites throughout Greece and Cyprus, and as far abroad as Russia, Romania, Ukraine, Egypt and the Holy Land.

There was also—perhaps most moving of all to those who knew him personally—his fervent desire to gather his spiritual children together in a community of love, "as a hen gathers her brood under her wings." (Lk. 13:34) And likewise, there were the countless instances in which words he spoke to his spiritual children were only later, after his repose and in the light of both private circumstances and public events, recognized as nothing short of prophetic.

Both translators of this present volume had the great blessing and privilege to know Fr. Daniel—if for far too short a time—as an inspirational figure and a beloved spiritual father. Fr. Nicholas Palis first met Fr. Daniel in 1970, when he visited Mt. Athos as an eighth-grader. Fr. Daniel became instrumental in Fr. Nicholas' path to the holy priesthood, providing him with spiritual counsel, and sending him spiritual books from Greece until the very end of his earthly life. Damian Robinson was a spiritual child of Fr. Daniel's from early 2007 until the elder's repose on July 11, 2009.

We would be remiss in closing this translators' foreword without mentioning a few brief technical points about the book. This translation is based on the third Greek edition of Fr. Daniel's book, which he published in Athens in 1985. In the present volume, we have attempted to maintain—insofar as was possible without trampling upon the rules of English grammar and syntax—the elder's writing style.

We have also tried to make use of photographic images and illustrations from the original book in order to keep the translation as close as possible to something that Fr. Daniel would have recognized. At times, this required us to sacrifice image quality, and we wish to apologize in advance for instances in which some photos are not as clear as we would have liked.

Last but not least, for the benefit of those readers to whom the various references in the text to different Greek localities, traditions and events might not have been familiar, we have incorporated a number of footnotes aimed at clarifying them or providing context. We hope these will add to a deeper understanding of the text, and that they will not distract the reader too much from the flow of Fr. Daniel's own words.

⁖ ⁖ ⁖

In presenting this translation of *The Miracle of Faith*, it is our fervent hope and prayer that Fr. Daniel's words be fulfilled in the hearts and souls of all who read this small offering of love—namely, that "having been sparrows, (they) will become eagles" and soar through heavenly places on the wings of indomitable faith!

Fr. Nicholas Palis and Lawrence Damian Robinson
Feast Day of the Holy Great Martyr Euphemia
July 11, 2014

PROLOGUE

"One thirsts for faith like 'parched grass'."
—Fyodor Dostoevsky[2]

When the fire in the fireplace is going out, it is fed with wood and brought back to life. Faith is a sacred fire which, when in danger, needs strengthening, so that it is not lost and the human breast become cold and empty.

Woe, if the flame goes out and gives way to the darkness and chaos of unbelief! More tolerable is the sky without stars, or spring without flowers, than a person without faith and hope.

Thus in order for the fire to be strengthened, we have published the following homilies, which were delivered at different times to various audiences and which were received with interest. May they reveal to some souls how powerful and fascinating the miracle of faith is.

---

[2] From Dostoevsky's January 1854 letter to Natalya Fonvizin.—*Ed.*

To whomsoever helped us in the publication of the present text (and there are quite a few of them) by supplying relevant information, by providing books, publications, icons and photographs, by translating foreign language texts, etc., we express our great gratitude.

—*Archimandrite D. Gouvalis*

First Homily

It is very customary for the Church to recommend that Christians attain to one virtue or another, and to urge them to this or that Christian duty. But it is also common for many people to remain, as a rule, unmoved by the exhortations of the Gospel. The beautiful world of piety and of morality attracts them very little.

What can the cause of this phenomenon be? What explanation can be given?

Many causes may exist, but the most basic one, I think, is this: the lack of faith. If one does not believe in God, why should he struggle to become sincere, just, or patient? What is the reason for one who does not accept the spiritual life, nor spiritual enjoyments, nor a future eternity "in the grace of Christ," to fight against and tame the passions of the flesh? For him, the unbeliever, the motto is: "Let us eat, drink and be merry, for tomorrow we die."

In other words, it is as if you were to urge a thirsty person to go to the next mountainside over in order to drink water from some spring, at a moment in which he does not believe at all that there is a spring in that location. For him there are springs and running water in other places.

Faith is also whatever the foundation is—whatever the first floor of the building is. If those things are missing, it is foolish for there to be talk about building the rest of the floors.

This homily of ours aims at nothing other than the strengthening of faith. Just as we have need of fortifying foods for the sick, we also need strengthening foods and vitamins for unbelievers and those of little faith.

✦ ✦ ✦

When we enter into a room or an office and we see an exceptional painting on the wall across from us, we admire the work and are ready to ask about the name of the great artist who painted it. And naturally there is no reason for us to think that this work of art does not conceal some creator behind it.

If we now turn our eyes ponderingly on the natural

world that surrounds us, we have unparalleled works of art to encounter. It is enough merely to take a walk in the springtime in a flowering meadow. Seeing so many flowers, with their wonderful compositions of colors, shapes and fragrances—not to mention their numerous varieties—we are uplifted.

We also experience the same thing with the very beautiful feathers of birds. What should one mention here first? The goldfinches, the pheasants, the exceptional peacocks, the exotic firebirds? The parrots? Indeed, that parrot which is called the "macaw" is a masterpiece: purple and red, with the neck and the lower part of the back light green, with its large wings yellow, blue and green, and some of the feathers of its long tail red and others blue.

And the hummingbirds? These, of which there are about five hundred species, are tiny little angels—microscopic "bird-flies" that fly from flower to flower to sip the nectar with their beaks. As they reflect the sun's rays on their scaly feathers, they create flashes like precious stones—emeralds, sapphires, diamonds....

And the birds of paradise? The beauty of these is beyond description. Their colors are as if magical. They intoxicate and make anyone who beholds them ecstatic. And the chiefs of primitive tribes in some tropical countries like to decorate their headdresses with their feathers. "Varicolored birds, made from the phantasmagoric morning mist!"

Once again, observing the delicate and beautiful wings of the multitudinous insects, and especially the elegant and multicolored chitinous shells of beetles—such as the familiar ladybug, for instance—we are literally enchanted.

We feel the same thing observing the goldfish, the pearls, and the sea shells in the seas. Ah, sea shells! What colors and shapes! Round, oval, conical, spiral—similar to drills, towers, amphorae, spindles; with one opening or two openings; some smooth, others pointed, others with knobs, others thorny. Their beauty is enviable, and especially when it comes to shells from tropical seas. "Nature is enchantment, and a dream in beauty and grace!"[3]

And what should one say about coral and coral reefs? Bright colors, fantastic buildings in the depths! And even more so when it comes to branch coral—when, in other words, certain branches rise up like

---

[3] From "The Free Besieged" by famed Greek national poet Dionysius Solomos (1798-1857).—*Ed.*

fairytale towers or bell towers of up to two-hundred and fifty meters[4] above the sea floor! There are yellow corals and blue ones and black ones—and white ones when the *Anthozoon*[5] dies—but the most famous are the red ones.

Their beauty is complemented or rather multiplied by the fish, because wherever there is coral, fish with superb coloration live. Moreover, even their names point this out: angelfish, parrot fish, emperor fish, queenfish, coachmen[6] (with grey and white stripes), surgeonfish (yellow), squirrelfish (red), etc. What gorgeous fish!

With their flamboyant and multicolored raiment, with so many variations on the color scale, with contrasting spots, with striking stripes, with dichromatic bands, with barbs covered with spectacular filaments like feathers, with diverse and varied forms and shapes...they cause a novel fascination. And as they swim among the exotic colonies of coral, they create a captivating phantasmagoria. Insuperable beauty! A fairytale garden of miracles!

---

[4] Roughly eight-hundred and twenty feet, or a sixth of a mile.—*Ed.*
[5] A reference to the scientific name of the animal, which is of the phylum *Cnidaria* and the class *Anthozoa*.—*Ed.*
[6] The pennant coralfish is also known as the 'coachman'.—*Ed.*

The beauty of creation speaks to the artistic Mind of the Creator.

And what should one say about the other superb adornment of the deep, the sea anemones? You think that they are flowers, but they are animals—animals in the form of flowers—*Anthozoa*,[7] glued to the bottom of the sea.

---

[7] Like coral, they are of the phylum *Cnidaria* and class *Anthozoa.—Ed.*

From their mouths sprout innumerable tentacles, similar to the petals of chrysanthemums and exhibiting superb coloration. These exotic flowers (sea anemones, rose bulb anemones, etc.) with their varieties—about a thousand species—their sizes and shapes, and their exceptional colors, blanket the expanse of the deep with carpets of unprecedented color.

One cannot find words to describe these paradisiacal beauties. Our soul's world is shaken by a feeling of sacred majesty before such sights. How can we not see some incomparable divine Artist behind all of these things?

A European intellectual rightly said that the wings of a butterfly can crush an atheist. In South America moreover, there exist some butterflies of unbelievable beauty before which the brushes of the best painters that have ever appeared on earth pale. There are also light-emitting nocturnal butterflies that create indescribable phantasmagoria when they fly.

Another amazing thing: if one examines the wings of a butterfly with a microscope, he will see over a hundred thousand microscopic feathers sculpted with much beauty. This alone is enough for one to end up in hymns of glorification, and to cry out together with the famous astronomer, Kepler: "O, Great Artist of the cosmos! I gaze upon the works of Your hands with awe!"

⸎ ⸎ ⸎

We also confront similar miracles in the sounds we encounter in nature, and especially in the winged world. Who is not attracted by the superb melodies of the chaffinch, the bee-eater, the robin red-breast, the canary, the skylark, or the nightingale?

Moreover it can be observed that the tones are excellently matched with their natural surroundings. In other words, when the scene is joyous, so are the melodies. When it is shrouded by a melancholic twilight, the songs are also melancholic. When it has harsh characteristics, the chirping is also harsh.

Thus at the beginning of the day, when bursts of morning sunlight awaken the forest and the whole scene appears joyous and optimistic, joyful and cheery chirping is heard; whereas at night, when everything is steeped in darkness, the sounds issue forth mournfully. The owls, Scops owls, screech owls, and other nocturnal birds only know plaintive songs.

We dedicate more attention to this topic in a separate book.[8] Behind these realities, we detect an all-wise Mind, unrivaled in the subject of musicology.

❖ ❖ ❖

Let us now shift the field of our observation to the historical realm.

The study of human history leads to important findings. Peoples who respected spiritual and moral values became great. Those who violated them were wiped out. Nations that sought to rule over others by force destroyed themselves in the end. There is an expression that sums this up:[9] "They went after a hair and ended up with haircuts." World War II offers striking contemporary examples.

Whoever studies the history of Christianity is greatly strengthened in their faith. Its spreading accomplished miracles. How were twelve illiterate fishermen—twelve humble and unremarkable and timid people, whose hands dripped with the saltiness of the sea, unarmed and poor—able to go up against an armored Roman Empire? And how did Christianity

---

[8] Archimandrite Daniel Gouvalis, *The Miracle of Creation* (*Τα Θαυμάσια της Δημιουργίας*), Athens, 1983.

[9] As there is no precise English equivalent to this Greek folk saying, it has been translated directly and this explanatory sentence has been inserted into the original text.—*Ed.*

manage to prevail in the end and overcome idolatry despite all the persecutions, confiscations, imprisonments, exiles and the cruelest martyrdoms and bloodshed? How were the sheep able to defeat the wolves?

By the end of the first century A.D., Christianity stretched from India and Persia up to Spain and the British Isles—an unprecedented religiopolitical event. History does not have any other such phenomenon to show us. It remains unrivalled.

And let's take into consideration that an invitation to this new religion meant not very pleasant things: to admit that the leader of your faith suffered a dishonorable death by crucifixion; to walk a narrow path with strict commandments, such as, for instance, temperance, forbearance, tolerance, humility of spirit, the taking up of one's cross, meekness, love for one's enemies, and other difficult demands. And worst of all, you exposed your very own life to danger.

Moreover, some of the Christian dogmas, such as those about the resurrection of the dead or the creation of the world from nothingness, were completely unacceptable and unthinkable for the ancient Greco-Roman world. Yet despite all that, the haughty tree of idolatry was shattered and the tree of the Cross was planted as far as the ends of the earth.

The matter resembles the following: "The emperor with all his military might and weapons did not manage to subdue the barbarians, and some poor and naked fellow, on his own, without having even one spear, managed to go up against them and to defeat them." (J. Chrysostom)

And today the Holy Scriptures, the Christian Bible, have arrived at being translated into about 1,700 languages and dialects. How can one explain all these things if he rejects the supernatural component that the Christian faith hides within it?

✦ ✦ ✦

Again, if one wishes to do studies and research on the rites, the sanctifying practices and the mysteries of the Church[10], there will come moments in which he will face the very live presence of the divine power before him. There are cases in which people ready to die, sentenced without appeal by medical science, miraculously recovered their lives and their vitality through the energy of the Christian mysteries of Baptism, or Unction, or Holy Communion, while the doc-

---

[10] The term 'mysteries of the Church' refers to the holy sacraments.—*Ed.*

tors who happened to be attending these cases remained astonished.

The martyr-like contemporary priest, Fr. Dimitri Dudko, famous for his sermons in Saint Nicholas of Moscow, relates the following:

> *A woman physician comes to our church. About ten years ago she developed cancer of the stomach. The diagnosis was precise, but even with no diagnosis it was obvious that her last days were upon her. She vomited daily. The stench of death was about her. It was difficult to be near her. She accepted her disease humbly, obediently, as a true Christian. At work she was shunned. She was deprived of her children. Her husband left her. Sensing how close the end was, she decided to receive the sacraments of Unction and Holy Communion. It was then that the miracle occurred.*
>
> *After she'd been anointed and received communion, the vomiting ended immediately. The stench gradually disappeared, and the doctors declared her cured. She's alive and well today, and works once again as a physician. Had this occurred in earlier times it would have been written up in all the newspapers, but today only her acquaintances know about it, only those who see her all the time. But anyone can meet her and talk to her.*

She's not afraid of witnessing to this event before any-
one. A miracle in person, as they say. I don't think any-
one would dare to deny it.[11]

The next incident concerns a family I know. In the summer of 1976, they had gone on vacation to a mountain village in the area of Kalavryta. Numbered among them was a cute little three-year-old boy. One day, without anyone being able to determine the cause, his cheeks and head became swollen; his eyes sank and could barely be distinguished—a dreadful and grievous sight. And where was a doctor to be found? The distraught mother notified the grandmother, who was located in another neighborhood. She was keeping blessed oil from Holy Unction. They anointed the child with it and the miracle was not long in happening. The swelling began to subside, and after two hours it had completely disappeared.

Let us also mention a supernatural phenomenon that is connected with the Mystery of Baptism. It happened in 1980 at the Sacred Monastery of Hilandar—

---

[11] Father Dmitrii Dudko, *Our Hope*, YMCA-Press, Paris, 1975, pp. 143-144. English translation from Russian by Paul D. Garrett. In Fr. Daniel Gouvalis' original Greek text, the reference is cited as: "From the book: Dimitri Dudko, OUR HOPE -TRANSLATION 'Elafos' Publ. Athens, page 155."—*Ed.*

that is, at the Serbian monastery of the Holy Mountain.

A Serbian student from Belgrade named Peter Restovic, an atheist and unbaptized until he was nineteen years old, found the Faith and asked to be baptized at the monastery of Hilandar. As the service was taking place, a friend of his took a photograph. At the time he took the picture, God allowed something of the invisible grace of the mystery of baptism to be revealed. This appeared when the pictures were developed.

All of them observed with amazement and sacred awe that on the head of the newly-illumined sat a white dove! His emotions, as soon as he saw the photograph, were indescribable. This photograph happened to come into our possession, and we present it to the readers so that they too may enjoy this beautiful work of wonder.

Years ago (in 1951) in a village of the prefecture of Phokidos, Panourgias—it lies in the northern foothills of Mt. Gionas and is my own homeland—a house was being built, and the pious and elderly owner of the house immured a bottle of holy water in the wall of the ground floor. Twenty-five years passed by, and it

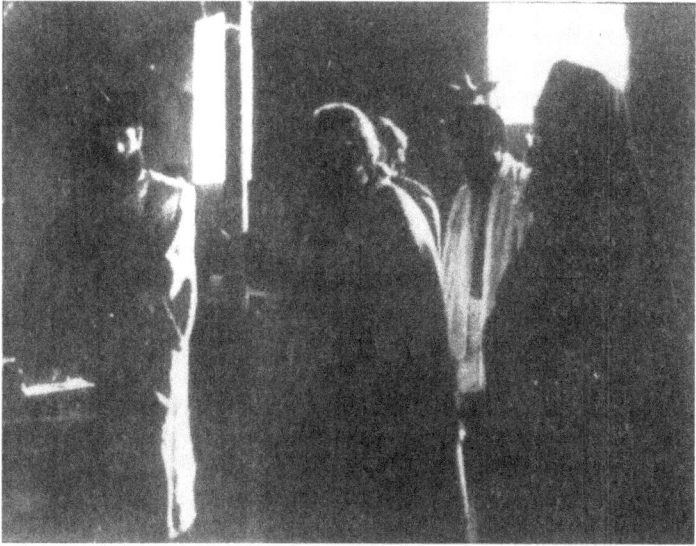

A dove on the head of a newly illumined (baptized) man.

became necessary to put a small window there. They happened to come upon the spot where the bottle of holy water was. And what did they see?

The blessed water was absolutely clear and clean, as if someone had taken it that very moment from the most cool and crystal clear spring. If the bottle had contained some other ordinary water, not only would it not have lasted 25 years, but I doubt if it would have lasted for 25 days.

In recent years, when the capital has become so filthy, many people remember their villages and look to find a plot of land there to build a house. And it has happened certain times—I have in mind specific incidents—that, while digging the foundation of the house, they find a bottle at a depth of one or one-and-a-half meters.[12] A curious thing.

They bring it up to the surface and examine it closely. It contains clear water. What in the world is going on, they wonder? How did it end up there? It must surely have been in that place for at least sixty or seventy years, because the property has been undisturbed for such a period of time. And how was it kept totally pure? Many questions.

Some old folks from the village, however, explain everything. Seventy years before, there were honeybee hives in that field, and the pious Christians in such areas were accustomed to putting holy water deep in the ground so as to bless and protect their beekeeping.

Many times home builders in large cities demolish an old two or three story house in order to put up a multistoried apartment building in its place. And as they are tearing down the four corners on the ground floor, they find four bottles full of water. It is holy water. They were placed there eighty or a hundred years ago. And the water is extremely clear. Whether

---

[12] About 3 to 4-1/2 feet.—*Ed.*

they want to be or not, they are left dumfounded.

In the village of Barnabas in Attica, which is very familiar to me because I often visited it as a preacher and confessor, they tore down a three-hundred-year-old house to replace it with a new one. And in one of its walls, low down, they found a bottle with very clear water. Naturally it was holy water. The construction workers were filled with surprise. Three hundred whole years and no deterioration, no change! That is the miracle of faith!

We could recount many things about holy water and the blessing of the waters. In the county of Sitia in Crete, a half hour outside of the village of Armenoi, there is a small cave that comprises a church dedicated to the Holy Spirit.

Whenever the little church celebrates its feast day, at the time when the Divine Liturgy is taking place, the roof of the cave becomes damp and a stalactite begins to drip. Thus a small cavity which is on the floor slowly fills up. It is holy water with therapeutic powers. Many sick people gain their health thanks to it.

If this miracle does not take place some year, it is because of some impiety or sinfulness of the pilgrims. For this reason the Christians take care to come with great piety. Certain times, when there is some need for the holy water, the Christians go to the chapel (as a rule they send little children, as they are purer) and they say the Creed three times. And it does not take long for the sanctified droplets to appear.

The last thing we will mention about blessed waters transports us to Limnos. In the northeastern part of the island is the small village of Plaka. One-and-a-half kilometers[13] away, you find the country chapel of Saint Charalambos. Wondrous miracles are told about its construction, which we will not narrate in the present text.

At a distance of about four-hundred meters, near the sea, there are four or five springs which issue the holy water of the Saint. A small shrine of his is set up there. The waters create a small mud pit, and from there the people of Limnos are supplied with sanctified mud, which they spread crosswise on the suffering members of their bodies to heal them.

Someone gets a dreadful headache. "Oh," his family members say, "what a shame! We're out of the mud bath of Saint Charalambos! We have to go and get

---

[13] Roughly one mile.—*Ed.*

some more." A person I know was suffering from paralysis, and with the "mud bath" of the Saint he was healed. Whoever is interested in more details can ask someone from Limnos.

Some years ago (in 1968) I happened to serve in Thessaly, in the Metropolis of Trikkis and Stagon. At that time, in a village called Nomi on the Thessalian plain, where the inhabitants were very involved with the cultivation of cotton, something very unpleasant was discovered. For the first time on record, a green worm appeared on the cotton blossoms—something which meant the complete destruction of the harvest.

Since it was something unprecedented, they did not know what pesticide to use in this case. They would have to send a sample to the appropriate government ministries which, after the necessary research and experiments to ascertain which drug could exterminate the enemy, would subsequently manufacture it and send it to them. But by the time all that research was done, it would already have been far too late.

For that reason therefore, the faithful Christians thought of something else. Headed by the priest of the village, by the name of Fr. Stephen, they performed a litany and supplication service in the middle of the fields, asking for help from above.

The litany and the petitions finished, and then something miraculous took place: there appeared flocks of very numerous sparrows, which poured into the fields and, flying from cotton plant to cotton plant, did not leave even one single worm alive. They wiped out all of them. The pious villagers did not know how to express their joy and their gratitude to God for such a quick response to their prayers.

Similar and even more impressive is the miracle associated with Kymi, the beautiful city located on the eastern shore of Euboea. In this city, a great religious celebration takes place every year on the 6th of May[14] with a large gathering of people and lively displays of worship. It also reminds everyone of an incredible miracle that took place about fifty years ago.

Innumerable locusts fell upon the area and threatened to destroy everything. The pious Kymians then asked the Monastery of Domvous, in the prefecture of Voiotia, for the skull of Saint Seraphim; they gathered at the Church of the Prophet Elijah, which is built on a

---

[14] The feast day of St. Seraphim the Ascetic of Mt. Domvous.—*Ed.*

small picturesque hill, and they held a vigil, a divine liturgy, a holy water service, and a procession with a great number of holy icons and the skull of the Saint, whose celebration was on that very day.

And then something happened that no one could have imagined: the locusts, as if pushed by an invisible power, gathered together and rose up in the air—a veritable cloud—and all rushed into the sea, where they drowned. The Christians did not allow such a miracle to be forgotten. Thus they established its festive annual remembrance.

It is not unusual for extraordinary phenomena to be observed in the actions and deeds of pious priests. Something related to this also happened to the virtuous and zealous clergyman, Fr. Gervasios Paraskevopoulos.

The pine tree he planted in Prophet Elijah of Patras was marked with a supernatural sign. It is something astonishing. Inside its trunk, across its entire length, a beautiful and artistic cross was formed, and with a much more intense appearance than the rings of the tree, to be sure. As soon as this was discovered, the pine tree was cut into numerous sections and distributed as a blessing to the Christians.

A cross formed inside the trunk of a pine tree.

After the pine tree, the myrtle tree. In Venerato, Crete, near Heraklion, at the historic Monastery of the Panagia of Palianis, you encounter a huge myrtle tree hundreds of years old. It is so large that it can give shade to 200 people. It resembles an enormous bouquet. All of its main branches are at an equal distance from the trunk. With the projection of the side branches, crosses are formed with rectangular precision.

Over the years, its trunk enclosed within it an icon of the Panagia, which had been found in its branches. They would take it to the church and it would return to the branches of the tree. And thus the whole tree was filled with the grace of the Mother of God.

This blessed tree exhibits quite a few supernatural things. The Christians cut little leaves and boil them. Then they drink it and are healed from various illnesses. As Abbess Marina informs us:

"Sick people use its leaves as an infusion. They drink it while fasting and bathe their hurting heads or other ailing body parts with it. Many housewives put them on flour kneaded with plain water and make leaven. The sisters always keep little branches with them as a blessing and for protection, and if they are traveling and the sea gets rough, they throw them into the sea to stop it."

Certain wondrous things also happen with the myrtle in relation to a thorny climbing plant—the "one without a bed,"[15] which produces bright red grape-like fruit in the winter—that has sprouted in the bouquet of the myrtle tree.

On September 24, the feast of the *Panagia Myrtidiotissa* (the All-Holy Virgin of the Myrtle Tree), innumerable crowds gather at this pilgrimage site. Over one hundred and fifty "blessing of the loaves" services take place. When the myrtle is in bloom, swarms of honey bees visit it and make the whole tree buzz, while at daybreak the wild birds in its branches chant their early morning prayers and doxologies.

We could also take note of some miracles sur-

---

[15] The common name of the plant, *Smilax aspera*, is 'ακρέβατο' (*akrevato*) in Greek, which literally means 'without a bed'. The related American variety, *Smilax regelii*, is commonly known as 'sasparilla'.—*Ed.*

rounding the breaking of ecclesiastical customs. Let's have a look at the custom of fasting, and let's transport ourselves to Crete, to the county of Sitia.

There, in the village of Lithines, is a very ancient church of the Panagia that celebrates on the 8th of September. On the iconostasis, in between other old Byzantine icons of marvelous technique, the "Panagia of the Lithines," which is surrounded by innumerable offerings, stands out. Its wonderworking efficacy is something else. We will only mention the miracle related to fasting.

It is the period of Lent, and some Christian goes to the store to buy meat. To take a shortcut and get home more quickly, he passes through the courtyard of the church. (The church has a large courtyard, as well as a hostel, at its disposal.) As soon as he gets home, he opens the package and what does he see? The meat has produced maggots!

This also used to happen in olden times. As soon as the person holding the meat would come out of the courtyard of the church, he would see it already full of worms. In more recent years, some unbelievers would buy the very freshest meat and pass by the yard of the church with it during the period of the Fast, only to

The Holy Myrtle

The Myrtle's hist'ry,
Divine tree of Palianis,
Is lyricized briefly
For the pilgrims.

Before the monastery was built
To all the side of this mount,
As they were saying it was forest,
They set fire round about.

When the flames arrived
At an aged bush,
"No! No!" in interruption cried
A commanding voice.

In fear they put out the flame,
Curious they investigate;
An icon they ascertain,
They bow down and venerate.

They made a worship place
On the spot, the villagers,
And the icon that had grace
They placed it gently there.

Within the Myrtle's limbs
The Virgin's form
Aloft was glimpsed—
Thus had it been drawn.

The school's little lasses
Often heavily censed
The icon, oh-so blessed
So it would enlighten them.

A miracle happened one day
To the children without sins
And real did become
Their sketches of the limbs.

In bunches they did plant them,
The little girls with gladness,
The branches that they plaited;
And they shot up with boldness.

A church a little further down
The villagers did build.
They transferred the icon
But away from there it fled.

Three times did they lock it,
It is said, inside the church;
The next day they did find it
In the Myrtle's branches perched.

It made them to comprehend
How it was not again allowed
For the icon to be rent
From its very own boughs.

Thus here inside it is found,
The trunk, the many-bough'd,
The same from which it did sprout
And which is a tree most hallowed.

Of divine grace it has partaken,
And for that everyone of faith
Takes its leaves or its branches
To be quickly made safe.

At the Holy Monastery of Palianis, September 24, 1940
Offering of the lowliest nun Theotimi

discover to their great surprise that it had become maggot-infested. It should be noted that the worms are conspicuous.

A certain unbelieving butcher tried his hand at passing by with half a lamb. In the middle of the yard his legs became paralyzed and he fell down with frightful shouts!

Let's remember the Greeks abroad a little, as well, and turn to Iowa in the United States. There, in Mason City, there is a Greek Orthodox Church dedicated to the Transfiguration of the Savior. In the year 1983, on the 5th Sunday of Lent, while the pious priest, Fr. Constantine, was celebrating the Divine Liturgy, a fragrant liquid began running from the holy altar table—something which greatly moved the entire congregation.

More specifically, on the holy altar there were two candelabras made of pure brass, each with five white candlesticks. As the Divine Liturgy of St. Basil the Great began and the "Petitions of Peace" were being said, something appeared to flow from the base of the left candelabra. The priest and the altar boys were taken by surprise. The candles were new. They had just lit them, and there was no chance that they had melted and were dripping.

They approached to examine it and saw that it was quite a cold liquid, like ice, and amazingly fragrant. Not even the choicest incense would have competed with it in fragrance. It was an unprecedented holy water. Little by little, something like a little stream formed, and it did not stop flowing for forty-eight hours.

The priest announced it to the packed congregation after the Gospel reading. Joy, tears, amazement, shouts of wonder! As they looked at it, venerated it and later put it into containers, they were filled with unheard of emotion. They anointed sick people with it and they regained their health.

The heterodox and people of other religions heard the news. They also ran to the church, bringing sick people who were also healed. The next Sunday, Palm Sunday, a fragrant liquid also sprang forth from the candelabra on the right. The church has now ceased being a simple parish church. It has become a pilgrimage site which makes the Orthodox rejoice.

Many times, supernatural signs are linked with important days, such as for instance with the great holidays of Christianity. Thus every year on the day of Theophany various "signs" occur. We will mention one.

In Cephalonia, at the Monastery of Saint Gerasimos, something very impressive happens at the reliquary where his relics are kept. As soon as the matins of Theophany begins, the entire reliquary gives forth an aromatic liquid like sweat! When the Divine Liturgy begins, it gushes forth more abundantly. And as the "Through the prayers..."[16] is heard, it stops. They gather this fragrant liquid and use it for holy water and for healing.

This strange sacred occurrence has been happening from very old times. A friend who had visited Saint Gerasimos around 1950 was telling me that, together with the sarcophagus, an icon of Saint Spyridon on the wall by the left chanter's stand also poured forth globs of sweat. (According to tradition, Saint Gerasimos himself had rendered this icon.) Furthermore many teardrops would run from the eyes of Saint Spyridon, and the faithful would gather them up with handkerchiefs and cotton. I have been informed that in recent years this miracle has stopped happening.

---

[16] In the Greek Orthodox tradition, the phrase "Through the prayers of our holy Fathers, Lord Jesus Christ our God, have mercy on us and save us" is the characteristic closing line of the various liturgical services.—*Ed.*

✢ ✢ ✢

Let's go now to the Holy Land—there where the prophets, the Panagia, the Apostles and the Lord walked.

The Resurrection service, in which the priest lights his candle from the vigil lamp of the Sanctuary and, chanting the "Come, receive the light!", distributes the paschal light to the faithful, is known to all of us. This service comes from the one which occurs every Holy Saturday in the Church of the Resurrection in Jerusalem. Things take place there which shake the souls of Christians. Let's observe them.

The people who throng together are very numerous. Many grab a spot in the church from the evening of Holy Friday. From the morning of Holy Saturday, the church is completely packed both inside and out— a suffocating crush. You even see people who have climbed up into the windows and wherever there is the tiniest space.

A little after 11:00 a.m., the tomb is sealed with a beeswax candle which was used in forty Divine Liturgies. Two huge white ribbons in the form of an "X" cover the door of the All-Holy Sepulcher—a representation of a related event which the Gospels mention.

After a little while, the sacred clergy enter the church. They wear their priestly vestments, and in a majestic procession they head from the Royal Doors of the church to the *"Kouvouklion"*[17] of the Holy Sepulcher, processing three times around in litany, while the hymns *"Angels in the heavens hymn Your Resurrection, O Christ Savior,"* and *"O, Gladsome Light"* resound.

Afterwards, the clergy return to the holy bema,[18] except for the patriarch and one archpriest (the latter will later take—first among the Orthodox—the Holy Light from the Patriarch to transfer it to the church, borne aloft, according to custom, on the shoulders of the faithful). The Patriarch takes off his external vestments, remaining in his white tunic—the so-called *sticharion*, a symbol of the white-garbed angel of the Resurrection—his belt, and kneepads. He proceeds towards the door of the sacred *Kouvouklion*, which as we said has been sealed with ribbons and wax.

As envisaged in the rubrics, a policeman searches him in case he has matches or a lighter with him. The

---

[17] A ceremonial canopy, often domed, over an altar or altar table, throne, or entry way, either suspended or supported by posts or columns. In the Latin Christian traditions, it is sometimes known as a *baldaquin.—Ed.*

[18] The raised platform with steps that communicates between the holy sanctuary and the nave of the church.—*Ed.*

time is precisely 12:00 noon. The door opens. He enters the Holy Sepulcher and, kneeling, recites certain prayers from a special booklet that was previously placed on top of the tomb. These revolve around the concept of the light that defeats the darkness. For example, "You, O Lord, who became man and brought a shining light to the people that walked in darkness. You who descended into Hades and filled with heavenly light the earthly and netherworldly places...."

Everyone waits in suspense. And all the candles and the vigil lamps—everything—are extinguished. The crucial moment approaches. A mysterious silence is spread over the whole congregation. If the wait becomes long, the crowd gets anxious and continuously cries out the "Lord have mercy" in awe. Everyone's gaze is turned towards the door of the *Kouvouklion.*

In an instant, supernaturally and miraculously, the Holy Light springs forth from the Sepulcher—"light shining forth from the tomb"—lighting first the holy vigil lamp that is above the tomb in a golden holder. In a text from the twelfth century, there is the characteristic phrase: "A new and heavenly light, on every holy Saturday, ignited the vigil lamps above the life-bearing and divine tomb."

Having read certain prayers, the Patriarch lights the four bundles of thirty-three candles each in order to then impart the sacred light to the thousands of Christians who receive it with ineffable emotion, with semantrons,[19] with bells, with chanting, with shouts, with cheers, with whistling.... Cries of joy... An ocean of divine rejoicing... A delirium of indescribable enthusiasm.

The more expressive Arab Orthodox in particular exhibit such an outbreak of enthusiasm that they turn the world upside down. Moreover, young people from Bethlehem, in accordance with long-established tradition, on top of one another's shoulders in the shape of a pyramid, sing the encomia[20] of the Holy Light in chants and whistles, with an impressive refrain: "Christ is ours! He was born in our city!" The atmosphere vibrates with otherworldly grace and glory. The human tongue is incapable of describing it.

The sacred sepulchral light is not only distributed by the Patriarch, but it also acts on its own. It appears outside the Tomb, with a particular hue completely

---

[19] A flat metal bar that is usually hung up in a monastery courtyard and is struck with a mallet in a rhythmic pattern to announce the start of church services.—*Ed.*
[20] Stylized hymns of high praise.—*Ed.*

different from any known light. It radiates, runs like a dove or like lightning around the Sepulcher. It flutters in between its vigil lamps. It vanishes and reappears, lighting some of them. Certain times it completely engulfs it, as if it has caught fire.

It flies like a bird inside the Church of the Resurrection, as well. It also goes to certain chapels, such as, for example, that of Golgotha or of the Cross, and lights their vigil lamps. It also lights the candles of certain Christians (everyone as a rule is holding thirty-three white candles). There are pious pilgrims to whom, as many times as they have attended this service, the holy light has come on its own and lit their candles! And they might be located very far from the *Kouvouklion.*

The spectacle is not independent from the degree of faith. One Christian might see the Holy Light as lightning, another as the flames of a furnace, another as a bright star that descends towards the sacred *Kouvouklion.* When the Patriarch comes out of the Tomb and, full of emotion, distributes the Holy Light, it might still be roaming above his head in between the vigil lamps.

Everything is flooded with light. Every last corner

of the huge Church of the Resurrection has been illumined. "Now everything has been filled with light." This is "the torch-bearing of the vigil lamps of the heavenly light of the holy Resurrection," according to the phrase of the ancient bishop (Basil of Emesa[21]—9th century). Of course, not only of the vigil lamps. It is a torch-bearing with a heavenly, extraordinary light not made by hands.

This God-given light exhibits unusual characteristics. As soon as it first appears, it has a coloration like azure—that is, completely different from ordinary light. A certain author speaks of "a mysterious blue light that moves and changes form." Afterwards, as it flies here and there, it gives the impression that it is something living, which decides on its own where it will go.

And furthermore, as soon as it first appears, for the three first minutes (exactly the three first minutes by the clock) it does not burn. You can touch it to your hands, your chest, your forehead or your mouth for a blessing, without anything happening to you. It does not burn at all.

---

[21] The present-day city of Homs in western Syria.—*Ed.*

"Come receive the light from the Unwaning Light!" The great moment has arrived. After the miraculous lighting, the blessed Patriarch of Jerusalem, Diodoros, distributes the fire to the faithful people, who glofrify God for His blessing to our Orthodox race. (Source: *Ecclesiastical Truth*, May 3, 1984)

If there are impressive sights, without a doubt the next one is numbered among the first. You find yourself at this sacred time in the Church of the Resurrection and observe a venerable priest with a very ample beard take his thirty-three candles with the Holy Light and touch them to his forehead, to his face and then— listen!—pass them in the form of a spiral through his beard and not suffer the slightest harm. If this were not a matter of the Holy Light, not only thirty-three, but not even one single candle could get near his beard without you understanding what was going to happen!

Once, some decades ago, the Greek Orthodox monk who guarded the Holy Sepulcher, desiring to clear up some troubling doubts of his, dared to hide in the sacred *Kouvouklion*, in a place across from the Holy Sepulcher, high up, behind the parapet supporting the vigil lamps. When, at midday on Holy Saturday, the Patriarch entered alone to receive the sacred light, he observed everything unseen.

As he himself related to us, his eyes encountered the most enviable sight. When the Patriarch bent to enter into the place of the holy Tomb, and while deathly silence prevailed everywhere, he heard a gentle whistling as if a light wind was blowing. Subsequently a sublime blue light filled the whole area of the Life-Giving Tomb. Afterwards, it moved with turbulence and awesome power. The subtle breeze changed into a type of violent whirlwind.

The Patriarch was kneeling before the All-Holy Sepulcher. At one moment, he took the booklet from the Tomb and began reading the prayers by the illumination of that pale-blue light, which had calmed down somewhat. Thick drops of sweat rolled down his face. Then that sacred light began a new swirling with indescribable speed and power. And from light-blue it transformed into the purest white, all white.

After that it took the shape of a solar disc that stood full of radiance above the head of the Archpriest. He took in his hands four bundles of thirty-three candles each, which he had previously touched on top of the holy Tomb, and he began lifting them upwards, as if he were saying, "My God, light them!" He did not manage to get them to the height of his head, because at the same moment they and the holy vigil lamp lit up, while the all-white sun vanished. Now the Patriarch, full of divine joy and satisfaction, came out towards the antechamber to impart the God-given light.

Such a sight could never be erased from the memory of the monk. It always stood out in his mind. "I saw the heavenly blue light in front of me everywhere," he confessed. "I saw it swirling restlessly, alive. I saw its dizzying turbulent movement everywhere. I heard its subtle and piercing whistle everywhere. Its subtle breath touched me. The invisible gentle breeze of its presence refreshed me...."[22]

Here, without doubt, we are dealing with a gift "coming down from above from the Father of lights."[23] No human action or skill can offer us such a light. It comes not from the material world, but from the world where the unsetting Light reigns, "from whom (comes) every light and to whom every light is darkness."[24]

Let us also note the following: it only appears through the invocation of the Orthodox archpriest. Whenever the heterodox have endeavored to seek

---

[22] Archimandrite Sava Achilleos, *I Saw the Holy Light*. Athens: 1982, pp. 127-129, 131-132.
[23] From the dismissal prayers of the Divine Liturgy of Saint John Chrysostom.—*Ed.*
[24] A quote from the Blessed Augustine.

after it, they have failed.[25] One time (in 1579) when the Armenians bribed the Turks and their own Patriarch entered into the All-Holy Tomb, while the Orthodox one stood sorrowfully outside the Church in front of a pillar, the light tore through the pillar and appeared to the Orthodox. Moreover, the Arab emir, Tounom, chief of the guard overseeing the services at the Church of the Resurrection, saw it from a neighboring minaret, with the result that he immediately abandoned Islam and embraced the faith of Christ.

---

[25] In the year 1101—at that time when the Holy Land had come under the Crusaders (Latin Rule*)—the Holy Light emerged after one day's delay, and only after the Roman Catholics departed from the service. In this regard, in *The History of the Church of Jerusalem* (p. 426-7), Chrysostom Papadopoulos reports: *"In 1101, an odd episode happened that shook up the Latins. A Latin eyewitness, Pulcherius, who later became Patriarch, relates that the Holy Light did not appear at all that year, despite all the litanies that were performed during which the 'Lord, have mercy!' was chanted by all those processing. 'We were overcome by very great sadness and grief. How many cries to the Lord! How many sighs, how many wailings! Because with wails we all chanted "Lord, have mercy!", so that through the chanting we might seek the mercy of the Lord; but even beseeching Him, we did not receive at all that which we sought....' The Holy Light did not appear, even on the morning of Pascha. King Baldwin, despairing, prayed before the Holy Sepulcher. The Latin clergy found itself in a very unpleasant position, not knowing if they should celebrate the feast of Pascha or not, without the Holy Light. Remaining in such an agonized condition, the Latins decided to depart from the Church of the Resurrection. However, the Greeks who remained in it became more fervent about the prayers.... They processed, they beseeched God and the Holy Light appeared, filling the entire Church. With shouts of joy, the Latins ran forward to receive the Light from the Hellenes. We repeat that this episode is related by a Latin eyewitness, as, in whatever way one would want to explain this, it is indisputable that the Greeks, humbled and scorned by the Crusaders, were uplifted through this. Thus from that time on, even during the time of the Crusaders, the service of the Holy Light remained as a clearly Greek service."* [*The 'Latin Rule' refers to the Latin Kingdom of Jerusalem (1099-1291).—Ed.]

It is also said that he drove three nails into the ground, crying out: "May nails thus be driven into anyone who denies that the Holy Light is true, and that there is one true faith—that of the Orthodox!" These things, however, inflamed the men of the guard, who grabbed him and burned him. He is considered a Christian martyr, and his relics, with signs of the fire, are preserved at the Monastery of the Great Panagia.

It should be noted that the split pillar—"the column divided by the light"—is still preserved, and that when the Orthodox enter the Church, they kiss it at the mark of the split. (See the related photograph on the next page.) A decree of the sultan from that time decided that only the Greek Orthodox would impart the holy light.

The appearance of the Holy Light is an event that takes place every year in front of thousands of eye witnesses—a momentous event. Because of this, the religious press also includes something in its columns every now and then. Here, as an indication, is a related report:

> *"With the presence of many hundreds of pilgrims from Greece and America, the Services of Holy Week and of Holy Pascha were celebrated in the Holy City this year,*

Pilgrims before the doors of the Church of the Resurrection.
The pillar split by the Holy Light can be distinguished.

with His Beatitude the Patriarch Diodorus presiding. The Fathers of the Holy Sepulcher offered their services to those attending church in the all-venerable Church of the All-Holy Sepulcher and in other sacred establishments. The gathering of a great crowd was observed during the service of the Washing of the Feet and especially

*on Holy Saturday at midday during the lighting of the
Holy Light, which occurred amidst the traditional cries
of joy of the locals and which appeared in a supernatural
manner, to the point where all those present were surprised and glorified the Resurrected Lord, because He
makes us worthy even today of such a benefaction, that
we perceive through the senses a real miracle, such as is
the origin, without friction or chemical or other means,
of the Holy Light."*[26]

There is no room for doubts and disputes. There is
only room to invigorate—and that of course to an ex-
aggerated degree—meager and weak faith. There are
moving cases of Jews who have believed in Christ because of the Holy Light, who were telling their fellow
countrymen: "Why are you waiting for the Messiah to
come? The Messiah came!"

⁜ ⁜ ⁜

With all of the above examples, and with numerous others that we could mention, the possibility is
provided for the foundations of our spiritual edifice to
be strengthened. Firm faith, strong and unshakable as
a boulder, granite-like, is the most precious provision

---

[26] *Ecclesiastical Truth*, May 1, 1982.

for the struggles of life. On the contrary, adherence to unbelief results in something disastrous. There is no man who is more in-secure, more up-in-the-air, or more unsupported than the unbeliever. It is as if he is walking on a floor with rotten boards.

If it is worth crying over anyone, it is the person without faith. "Woe to him who has lost his faith!" Faith comprises the anchor of hope, thanks to which the captain will not fear the onslaught of the storm. Faith, according to the words of a great Apostle, is a shield—"Take up the shield of faith, with which you can extinguish all the flaming arrows of the evil one"[27]—a great shield upon which the enemy's arrows break. And woe to whomever has lost this great shield!

Faith resembles a secret spring which brings forth the water of consolation and encouragement—with a heaven-sent sunbeam that chases away the black darkness. "I often stretched out my hand on sad nights," exclaimed a certain person with faith, "and I felt another hand squeezing it."

Faith "lifts up the downtrodden" and restores ruined houses. Faith means invincible power with

---

[27] Eph. 6:16—*Ed.*

which we leap over the thousand-and-one obstacles that show up in the course of our life. And to use the expression of the Theologian: "This is the victory that has overcome the world, even our faith."[28]

---

[28] 1 Jn. 5:4—*Ed.*

SECOND HOMILY

The difficult times we are going through have made sickly, or have completely withered, the tree of faith in many souls. Nevertheless there exist reservoirs from which abundant water may be drawn, so that the diseased and moribund tree might flourish again.

In the natural and historical space around us, events occur which speak of the existence of a majestic invisible world. If anyone approaches these realities with an unbiased look, it is like watering the atrophied plants of his soul with the most plentiful water. How truly moving it is for someone doing astronomical research, for instance, to ascertain behind the movements and the laws of the heavenly bodies the palpable existence of a wise—and even more, a loving—Creator, who has regulated every single thing with the utmost care and kindness!

But let's get more specific. Let's make a scientific

journey to the stars[29] closest to us and let's allow them to talk to us.

The sun comprises the center of a family of astral bodies. Nine[30] heavenly bodies, nine planets surround it and revolve around it constantly, like—to make an analogy—in olden times the horses on the threshing floors went around the post that was driven into the center of the threshing floor. One of those nine is also the planet that carries us on its back, the Earth.

The Earth is the only one which is inhabited by people. The other eight are deserted. And the position of the Earth is ideal, the most suitable. It is not too near the center, the sun, but it is also not too far removed.

On the surface of the sun there is a temperature of 4000° Celsius.[31] So if the Earth were located in the position of the planet Mercury or of Venus, it would resemble a blazing furnace. If, again, it was located in

---

[29] The term 'stars' is used here in a general sense (as in 'heavenly bodies') to also encompass the planets of our solar system.—*Ed.*

[30] In the nearly 30 years since *The Miracle of Faith* was first published in Greece, astronomers have discovered at least two more small planets (or planet-like bodies) in our solar system, and have reclassified Pluto as a 'planetoid'. These discoveries, however, do not materially affect the main points of Fr. Daniel's discussion.—*Ed.*

[31] Current scientific data supports that the sun's surface temperature is actually about 5500° Celsius, or 10340° Farenheit.—*Ed.*

the position of the planets Saturn, Uranus, Neptune or Pluto, it would resemble a dreadful refrigerator. In the first case we would roast. In the second we would freeze.

But even if it was located in the position of Mars—the order is the following, starting from the Sun: Mercury, Venus, Earth, Mars, Jupiter—again things would be bad. According to information that the spaceship *Mariner 4* brought back when it researched Mars quite a bit in 1964, this planet suffers from bitter cold at night, because the temperature descends to 73 degrees below zero—a freezing without precedent.[32] It was also determined that violent windstorms blow there.

These unpleasant things have been avoided on Earth, because our heavenly Father placed our planet in the most completely appropriate place, so that the temperature that comes from the sun arrives here in the most ideal intensity. It is something that perhaps we didn't know and didn't think about—the miracle of divine providence, a support to faith.

---

[32] Surface temperatures as low as -107° C (-161° F) have been recorded at the site of the Viking lander, while average temperatures of about -153° C (-243° F) are estimated at the Red Planet's polar caps.—*Ed.*

In the relationship between the sun and the earth we can discover other wonders as well. Let's study, for instance, the movement of the earth. It is known to all of us of course that the earth moves, both around its axis and it around the sun. Furthermore, in one year it marks out one rotation around the sun.

It has been measured that the earth moves at a speed of 1,760 kilometers per minute[33]—an amazing speed! Next to this, the speeds that even the fastest rockets produce pale in comparison. Let's examine this situation a little.

Why then is the speed so great? Couldn't it be less? If it were, for instance, 50 or 100 or 150 kilometers per minute, would anything unpleasant happen then? Certainly! And very bad things, moreover.

If, for example, the earth were traveling at 176 kilometers per minute, we would have a huge increase in the span of day and night. Day and night would not each be 12 hours long. They would be much longer— 120 hours!

Now imagine a hot summer day that lasted 120 hours. The burning rays of the sun would literally sow

---

[33] About 65,616 miles per hour.—*Ed.*

complete destruction on plants. They would burn up and wipe out the vegetation. The plant world would be on a course towards death. And when the world of plants was destroyed, anyone could understand what lamentable conditions it would mean for the animal world, as well. In other words, the earth would start to appear like the image of a graveyard.

And again, what can we say about a night that lasted 120 hours? It would be a proper torture for one to wait for the day to break.

Venus, our neighboring planet, moves at such a slow speed that one day of sunlight is the equivalent of 127 of our own. If something like that happened on our planet, our day and night would be 3,048 hours long. So you can understand what would happen down here!

The moon also hides some impressive realities in relation to the earth. Its distance from our planet fluctuates at around 380,000 kilometers[34]. This distance could very well be quite a bit less, exactly as happens with other planets that have their satellites very close by.

[34] Roughly 236,000 miles.—*Ed.*

Let's hypothesize then that it was 80,000 kilo-meters[35] away from us. In this case, one might say that we would benefit, because we would see better at night. Yes, but! We would be anything except better off. Twice every twenty-four hours, enormous tides would rise up in the oceans and the seas, and their huge waves would pour out onto dry land. And the sailors, the people of the seas, the inhabitants of coast-al areas, and the countries with a low elevation would face tragedies.

The consequences? Drowning, destruction and lamentations. The only solution would be for everyone to get up and take to the mountains. Nothing tragic happens, however, because Someone did a good job calculating the distance between Earth and its satel-lite.

Now let's turn our attention and make our obser-vations a little lower than the stars, in the region of the atmosphere.

Of the entire quantity of air the atmosphere has, if we separated it into 100 parts, 21 of these would com-prise the familiar and beneficial oxygen. There is some

---

[35] About 50,000 miles.—*Ed.*

mysterious mechanism, which the greatest scientists of atmospheric chemistry cannot figure out, which for thousands and tens of thousands of years now fixes it so that this percentage remains constant.

However there is the possibility that the amount could be larger or smaller. In these cases, what results would we have? If it were smaller—easy for one to understand—we would not have enough, we would not be able to meet our needs, and the danger of asphyxiation would threaten us.

But if it were larger? Perhaps one might say that things would be pleasant, because we would have enough and even an abundance of oxygen. Yes, but! The consequences would be grievous.

If, instead of 21 percent, we had a quantity of 22 percent, very unpleasant phenomena would follow. All of the combustible substances and materials of the earth would become excessively flammable and would catch fire with the slightest cause. Let's be even clearer: if lightning struck a tree in some forest, the whole forest would immediately catch on fire. It would be consumed by fire and would be turned into ashes.

If the 21 percent got closer to 30 percent, it is certain—as special studies (e.g., by British professor, J.

Lovelock[36], known for his studies in atmospheric chemistry), state—that all of the vegetation of the world would become a vast holocaust.

Thus even the amount of the gasses is calculated precisely—a miracle of the love and a message of the care of the wise Creator and Sustainer of the world. And this is perceived even more when one casts a glance at the neighboring planets—Mars, for instance.

The American *Viking* spacecraft informs us that this planet is comprised of a vast desert, without the slightest amount of grass, and without any organic molecules[37]. Its atmosphere is very thin—one-hundred times less than that of Earth; and as we said, very strong winds blow—something which is due to the thinness of the atmosphere, but also to there being great differences in temperature between the equator and the poles. And the most destructive thing for the capability of developing human life is that the atmo-

---

[36] James Lovelock, a leading British scientist and inventor, who proposed the controversial and influential 'Gaia hypothesis' in which the earth is considered to be a self-regulating system.—*Ed.*

[37] Analyses of the soil chemistry of Mars in 2013 by NASA's *Curiosity* rover has determined that simple organic molecules most likely do exist on the Martian surface; however it is not clear whether these molecules came from ancient microbial or purely chemical processes. This information was unknown at the time of the original publication of this book, and does not detract from the main points made by Fr. Daniel.—*Ed.*

sphere contains 95 percent carbon dioxide! Fortunately on our own planet all these evils are absent.

The care that has been taken for earthly life is worthy of wonder when the layer of ozone that exists in the higher strata of the atmosphere is examined. Ozone is a gas, blue in color, with a characteristic odor, every particle of which is comprised of three atoms of oxygen (the 'allotropic' form of oxygen, as chemists say). The ozonosphere surrounds our planet—a layer of ozone with a thickness which varies from five to ten centimeters[38]—and is a protective cloak of invaluable importance. This layer absorbs a mass of ultraviolet rays that come from the sun.

If something like this did not occur, the plant and animal life on earth would be destroyed by the biological effect of ultraviolet radiation. This radiation burns the cells of plant and animal organisms. It likewise causes coloration and burns on the skin, as well as ophthalmia,[39] a disease that leads to blindness.

Whatever amount of ultraviolet radiation passes

---

[38] About 2 to 4 inches.—*Ed.*

[39] Also known as ophthalmitis, this condition is symptomatic of many diseases of the eye, one of which is actinic conjunctivitis or actinic ray ophthalmia. The latter is caused by prolonged exposure to UV rays and is undoubtedly what Fr. Daniel had in mind.—*Ed.*

through the ozone layer is useful, because it contributes to an organism's tissues forming Vitamin D, which is necessary for the creation of bony skeleton. It should be further noted that the complete lack of ultraviolet radiation causes rickets.[40]

Everything is made with wisdom! Whatever is necessary passes through, and whatever is dangerous is blocked. Thus, in its own way, the ozonosphere speaks to the existence of an invisible love that protects the creatures of the earth from dangers.

Water, ice and snow also relate to the atmosphere. Let's turn the discussion to these a little, too. We'll begin with snow, which, when it falls and decks Creation all in white, constitutes an enchanting spectacle.

Whereas water is colorless, snow takes on a white color. And this is not by chance. It hides a wondrous purposefulness, of which we will also make note. Whatever is white radiates all the light it receives. Thus, by reason of its whiteness, snow also does not absorb but casts off the various rays—something which causes it not to melt quickly, but to water the

---

[40] Rickets, a disease caused by defective mineralization of bone which is especially prevalent among malnourished children, is primarily caused by a lack of Vitamin D (necessary for the proper absorption of calcium).—*Ed.*

earth very slowly and to fill the subterranean reservoirs with water.

If it had another color, it would warm up and melt at a quick pace, with the consequence of poor hydration of the ground, a decrease of cultivatable land and of the forests, a lessening of the deposits of groundwater, dangerous erosion and the creation of many floods. All these things are avoided because the snow is white.

Now let's pay attention to something of the utmost importance that is observed about water. This blessed element[41] exhibits something of the anomalous and unusual. And this anomaly comprises the most invaluable benefit for life on earth.

Whereas with other elements, when the temperature falls to zero, density increases, and when it rises from zero, density decreases; with water, the greatest density is observed at four degrees Celsius. At that temperature it has the greatest specific gravity (1.000). At zero degrees Celsius, despite being found in a solid state, it has a lower specific gravity (0.9998). Thus

---

[41] The term 'element' (στοιχείο in Greek) is used here and in the subsequent discussion figuratively. Chemically, water is actually a compound, not an element.—*Ed.*

when it freezes it floats, because it is lighter.

If this rare quality did not take place—if it were not lighter as ice—then woe to the inhabitants of the earth! The ice would fall into the depths of the seas. New ice that formed would be added to the previous layer, and so on.

The result would be that enormous mountains of ice would form in the seas, which would destroy sea life. That would disturb the ecological balance with destructive consequences for every living being on earth. Likewise, climatic conditions would be agitated.

And the poor sun! How would it manage to melt such huge masses of ice at such a depth? However, we are saved from all of these tragedies because Someone determined that water should be heavier in its liquid state at a few degrees above zero!

❖ ❖ ❖

After scientific things, we will turn our attention to other areas. Let's allow some other simpler facts to be put before us, upon which the hand of God appears in a particularly manifest and incontrovertible way.

The Formation of the Bush on Mount Sinai. In accordance with the narrative of Holy Scripture, God repeatedly appeared to Moses, the leader of ancient Israel, on the sacred mountain of Arabia[42], Sinai. The first time, moreover, he appeared as an exceedingly flashing fire upon a bush, which burned without being consumed— "aflame and not burned!"

In accreditation and commemoration of this event, God has sketched the bush on the rocks of Sinai, both on their surface and on their interior. You see that bush engraved in miniature on a stone. You break it, and you discover that the same thing occurs inside. On some of them it appears somewhat obscured, on others clear, and on others crystal clear. It is an amazing phenomenon.

Today, three or three and a half thousand years later, the visitor to the God-trodden mountain who sees these formations looks to take some rocks with him. As soon as the children of the Bedouins see pilgrims at the Monastery of Sinai, they supply themselves with many such rocks and go to sell them for

---

[42] The consensus of the vast majority of current Christian (and other) traditions is that the Mt. Sinai where Moses received the Ten Commandments is that mountain located on the Sinai Peninsula in Egypt (where the Greek Orthodox monastery of St. Catherine is situated). There are also, however, other more controversial theories asserting that it is actually a different mountain in the northwestern region of modern Saudi Arabia. The Apostle Paul, in the first century A.D., likewise apparently claimed that Mt. Sinai was in Arabia.—*Ed.*

four or five Israeli shekels each. (This of course is the case if the Sinai is under Israeli occupation, as it was when we visited in 1978.) Admittedly it is something that astonishes—an unprecedented case! There is no other mountain on land or sea where such an extraordinary phenomenon is observed.

If rocks are found somewhere with similar designs—scientists speak of pseudo-petrification "dendritis"—it can easily be ascertained that the Bush is

Formation of the bush in a rock from Sinai.

not depicted on these. The rocks of Sinai exclusively have the design of the Bush.

But there is something else as well. That ancient bush is still preserved behind the sanctuary of the monastery's church, and it blooms every year. In the entire vast area of the Sinai Desert, despite the fact that there are innumerable thorny plants, no other bush is found! Absolutely none!

The Wels Catfish of the Jordan. From Sinai let's move on to the Promised Land, to Palestine, and let's do some research on the sacred river where Christ was baptized and the worship of the Trinity was made manifest. In this river there live some large fish, one meter[43] long, called Wels catfish.[44]

Wels catfish are the largest of the freshwater fish, and they live exclusively in these waters. The Wels catfish—notes T. Potamianos—is a wild animal of the lakes, a stout beast, rapacious and insatiable! A large flat head, with little round eyes and with...six whisk-

---

[43] About a yard.—*Ed.*

[44] The Wels catfish (Silurus glanis), or 'sheatfish', is a large catfish native to central, eastern, and southern Europe and the Mediterranean. The second largest freshwater fish after beluga sturgeon, they have been reported to reach up to 4 m. (13 ft.) in length and 180 kg. (400 lbs.) in weight.—*Ed.*

ers. Two are located on the upper jaw and are huge. They serve as radio receivers, and offer it useful information.

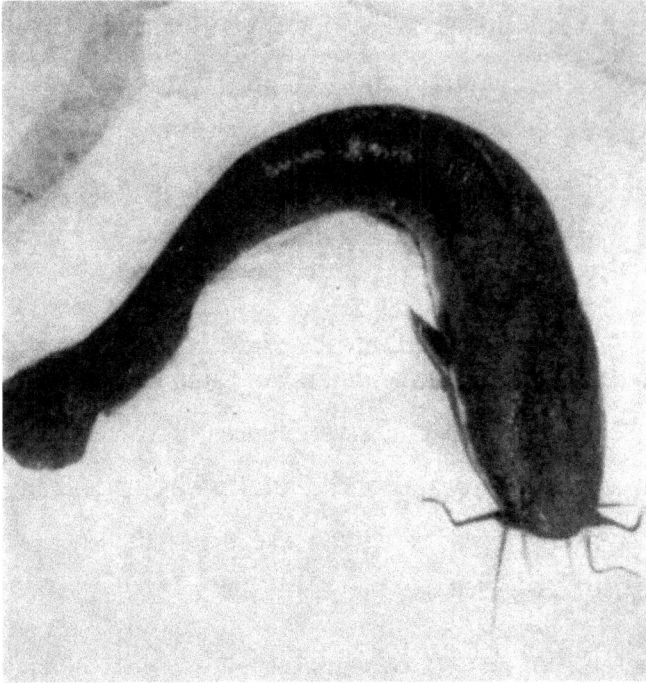

A Wels catfish from the River Jordan.

It has a well-like mouth with thin little teeth and a long narrow body, which is rather flat. Its fins are small, without barbs. Its skin is full of beautiful designs and arabesques that are reminiscent of autumn leaves, when the wind spreads them out on the ground. Its eggs are plentiful and significant.

In the lake of Castoria, there are Wels catfish that

surpass one meter in length and reach a weight of 40 kilograms.[45] They are voracious fish. They eat whatever they find—fish, worms, etc.[46] Their preference is worms.

They also have the exceptional ability to feel earthquakes ahead of time and, with sudden movements and circles in the water, to give a warning. They're living seismographs!

Of course, one encounters Wels catfish in different lakes and rivers, but a unique supernatural sign is observed in those of the Jordan. On their head, which is larger than one hand span, on the upper part, if we removed the flesh, we would discern an amazing representation in the bone. With various lines, cavities and projections, a human body is formed in the middle of the bone.

On the right and on the left one can distinguish the open wings of an angel, and above, very clearly and intensely, a dove with open wings. To the sides of the bird, on both sides, there are rays pointing downwards. In other words, the baptism of Christ is clearly

---

[45] Over three feet in length and 88 pounds in weight.—*Ed.*

[46] There have even been reports of especially large Wels catfish eating ducks and other water fowl, or leaping out of the water to catch low-skimming birds out of the air.—*Ed.*

depicted, just as ecclesiastical iconography represents it. And this happens only to the Wels catfish of the Jordan! It likewise happens in Lake Gennesaret[47], since that lake is formed from the waters of the Jordan.

Moreover, if the Israeli fishermen happen to catch a Wels catfish among the other fish, they throw it back into the lake. They do not want to eat it, because it is related to Christ. The pious pilgrims to the Holy Land consider it a great blessing to obtain a skull from these fish. And following that, they usually make the representation more intense by giving it the appropriate coloration.

The divine signs in the land of Palestine are very numerous. We will refer to one particularly grace-filled one that is related to Tabor, the mountain where Christ was transfigured in front of the three notable Apostles.

Situated in Galilee, this mountain has a height of 610 meters if we measure it from sea level, and 855 meters from the surface of Lake Tiberius,[48] and rises alone in the fertile Jezreel Valley. At its peak you find a

---

[47] 'Lake Gennesaret' is one of several names for the Sea of Galilee. Other names include 'Lake Kinneret' and 'Lake Tiberias'.—*Ed.*

[48] Roughly 2,000 feet above sea level, and 2,800 feet above Lake Tiberias, or the Sea of Galilee, which is the world's lowest freshwater lake.—*Ed.*

small plateau.

According to the Gospel narrative, at the moment when the Apostle Peter spoke to the transfigured and glorified Christ on the summit of the mountain, a luminous cloud descended and enveloped them all. And immediately, from within this sacred cloud, the very voice of God was heard.

In order for the faith of the Christians to reinforce that these things happened, but also for the ecclesiastical holidays to be sanctioned with God's seal of approval, every year an impressive miracle occurs on Tabor. In August, during the feast of the Transfiguration of the Savior, while the Divine Liturgy is being performed in the church of the Orthodox monastery at the summit of Mt. Tabor in the morning hours, a cloud comes down from the sky and covers the peak for a few hours. Only the peak.

As soon as the feast of the Transfiguration approaches, the Orthodox who are in Jerusalem and elsewhere make ready to go to Tabor. They long to see this godsent cloud, which will bring to their minds the "Behold, a bright cloud overshadowed them."[49] It is

---

[49] Mt. 17:5—*Ed.*

said that whoever is pure in heart sees this blessed cloud intensely in luminosity and splendor.

In our description of the Holy Land we will also include the Pool of Siloam, which is found in the southeastern corner of Jerusalem, below the area where the famous Temple of Solomon was built. Its water proceeds through in ancient stone aqueduct and forms the font of the same name. We know that Christ sent the man who was born blind here to wash and be healed.

Tradition mentions that in the 8th century B.C., when the Assyrians were besieging Jerusalem, an amazing miracle occurred following the prayer of the Prophet Isaiah. That is, when the foreigners approached the spring, the water diminished and dried up! When the Israelites went there, it gushed abundantly. It would abruptly stop and abruptly gush forth.

As a testament and a memorial to this miracle, something unique and exceptional, which cannot be explained by any natural cause, happens at the spring even today. Two or three times every 24 hours, the water stops running. And after every interruption, an hour having passed, the flow begins again abruptly and with a great quantity of water, which little by little returns to its customary regular flow.

Both the time periods between the interruptions and the amounts of water that come out after the interruptions are completely irregular and indeterminate—exactly as it was undefinable at that time, during the years of the siege, when the Jews would go to the spring to find a lot of water and when the soldiers of Sennacherib would go to find the least amount.

Tradition places the Prophet Isaiah's tomb near this spring.

The Holy Cave of Lebanon. Mount Lebanon, with its famous cedars, is known from the pages of the Bible. On one of its steep slopes, you encounter a cave with stalactites. In Arabic it is named *"grot kadisha,"* which means "holy cave." It's depth as you go in is endless. From its crevices issue streams of water that collect in an enormous pool of about 50 meters' depth[50] and, following that, pour out and plunge like a waterfall over the cliff.

The centuries have formed innumerable stalactites

---

[50] About 164 feet.—*Ed.*

and stalagmites there in a variety of shapes and sizes. The most impressive and amazing thing is that they have even formed the All-Holy Virgin with Child[51], in the midst of tapers and vigil lamps! Unbelievable but true!

Let's hear the words of an eyewitness, the ever-memorable Metropolitan of Karystia,[52] Panteleimon Phostini, that great and irreplaceable hierarch:

"For a moment one thinks that he is in an immense factory, where invisible hands carve divine works of art. The master craftsman is the water. And the water that drips from its walls and roof also works constantly, day and night for thousands of years now, and renders these ineffable masterpieces, which have been displayed as if in an inconceivable exhibit in the cave. What curious, what utterly marvelous compositions!

"On one side, the stalagmites have masterly formed a priest sitting on an arm chair. Further over, a life-size elephant has tossed his trunk down to the ground as if seeking something, while its enormous ears and its tusks

---

[51] Literally, the All-Holy (Virgin) as the One-Holding-the-Infant (in Greek, *Παναγία Βρεφοκρατούσα*).—*Ed.*

[52] Karystia was formerly a county within the province of Euboea, Greece, until it was merged into a larger county in a 2006 redistricting.—*Ed.*

complete the representation.

*"At a height, a statue of the Panagia[53] appears abso-
lutely clearly, holding Christ in her embrace and with
thousands of candlesticks—with stalagmites as their all-
white supernatural tapers—all around her, and up above
innumerable artistic vigil lamps—stalactites—of different sizes and shapes. The cave took on the name 'holy
cave' from the statute of the Panagia."[54]*

Divine providence even works with stalagmites
and water!

<u>Peeling Onions without Tears.</u> Ten kilometers south of
Kymi, on a beautiful little ridge, lies the village of
Oxylithos.[55] Its name is due to a pointy rock that rises
above the village. A lot of people gather there on
August 15th.[56]

Behind the ancient Church of the Dormition, a
lovely beef and onion stew is served at numerous ce-
ment tables—an old custom that they have kept even

---

[53] *'Panagia'* (literally 'All-Holy One') is one of the most common
appellations used by Greek Orthodox Christians for the All-Holy and
Ever-Virgin Mary.—*Ed.*

[54] Met. Panteleimon Phostini, *Struggles for the Fatherland in a Foreign
Land (Αγώνες για την πατρίδα στην ξενιτειά)*, Athens, 1954, pp. 192-193.

[55] Literally 'Acid Rock'. (No, this is not a joke.)—*Ed.*

[56] The feast day of the Dormition of the Theotokos and Ever-Virgin
Mary.—*Ed.*

The Church of the Dormition in Oxylithos.

in difficult times, such as during the Nazi Occupation. The meal is offered for free to foreigners. The bishop of the area is also present to bless the food and drink. Within the "drink" is also included a nice wine. Everything is delicious and blessed.

The blessing that is felt the most, however, is made manifest on the eve of the celebration, when numerous women of the village peel more than a ton of onions—onions for a hundred or more pots! Not one eye gets teary. They all know it. It is the blessing of the One Full of Grace. At home they might peel one or two of the same onions and the tears would come. Here they peel numerous sacks, and not one teardrop! A

On the day of the Dormition of the Theotokos (August 15th), "Stiphada" (a traditional beef and onion stew) is served on these tables in Oxylithos.

miracle—a miracle in the language of the people, very understandable and very impressive.

Something like this also happens at other celebrations of Orthodox churches. God sends many supernatural signs to the Orthodox people. For instance, at Kalyvia of Lavrio, at the chapel of the Archangels Michael and Gabriel, there is no problem of tears during the peeling of the onions for the stew. A relative of mine happened to do the peeling one time (November 7th, the eve of the feast of the Archangels), and he mentioned it to me when I said a word to him about the case of Oxylithos.

Salvation from Volcanoes. There are cases in which faith has neutralized the deadly threat of volcanoes. We will mention two miraculous events offhand.

In 252 A.D. in Sicily, an explosion of Mt. Etna formed a fiery river which flowed towards the city of Catania. The Christians then took the veil of the holy martyr Agatha from her tomb and stood across from the danger. And—an exquisite thing—the current of the lava respected the Saint's veil and turned backwards.

But let's come to more recent years, as well. In 1738, one of the volcanoes of Iceland erupted. (Let's note that Iceland, that large island with its strange geological composition and geysers, has around a hundred volcanoes, which are for the most part active). The violently boiling lava was going down towards the village of Vik.

At that critical hour, the pious priest of the village was in the church at the edge of the village. With fervent faith, he lifted up his hand and blessed it, and the lava—great miracle!—became motionless in front of the door of the church. The whole village celebrated the unhoped for salvation with ineffable emotion and religious awe. The dried lava remains at the entrance of the church until today as a living relic of the miracle, and thus proclaims the majesty of faith.

This miracle shook up Iceland and was documented officially in the pages of its history. We should also note that, here in Greece, in the *Illustrated History*,[57] it is recorded in detail in the article about Iceland. No one can dispute such facts.

The Great Miracle of Saint Menas.[58] We don't need to go to faraway Iceland to behold the supernatural grace of God, however. Miraculous events take place in our own homeland as well. In Heraklion, Crete, the patron saint is celebrated twice a year: on November 11th, which is his feast day, and on the Tuesday of Pascha.[59]

During the second festival, a hierarchical Divine Liturgy takes place in the ancient and historic church of the Saint. The whole church and the floor are decorated with myrtle branches and leaves. The time when the Gospel is read, when everyone is holding small lit candles in their hands—an offering from the church—is moving. After the Liturgy, a majestic procession

---

[57] *Illustrated History*, Papyros-Press, April 1970, p. 131.
[58] Saint Menas the Wonderworker was from near Memphis in Egypt, and was a high-ranking military officer. Leaving the army, he became a hermit for several years. Upon hearing a heavenly voice prophesizing his martyrdom, he returned to civilization, confessed his faith, and was martyred around 309 A.D.—*Ed.*
[59] Easter Tuesday, or "Bright Tuesday."—*Ed.*

takes place with resurrectional banners and with a procession of the relic of Saint Menas. Distinctive prayers and petitions are heard during these manifestations.

Why all this? To commemorate the great miracle that Saint Menas performed in 1826, on the night of Pascha (April 18th).

At the moment the Christians were celebrating the Liturgy in the church, the Turks raided in a frenzy to slaughter them (they found them all gathered together and without weapons—an opportune occasion!), whereupon Saint Menas appeared on horseback with his sword and drove them off. Moreover, he appeared in the form of a high-level Turkish officer and shouted at them that the command for the slaughter had been rescinded. They returned to their homes, and the Christians were saved.

The next day both the Christians and the Turks realized that the Saint had intervened. Because the miracle happened at the time when the Gospel was being read, they now have the custom of everyone holding lit candles at the time of the Gospel, as we previously mentioned.

The Intervention of Saint Charalambos.[60] A certain miracle of Saint Charalambos, which happened in 1944, is particularly impressive.

In the southeast Peloponnese, in the county of Trifylias, there is a picturesque city of 9,000 inhabitants, called Philiatra. Saint Charalambos is the patron saint of the city, and every year on February 10th a large celebration takes place in his honor. Even the people from Philiatra who live in Athens go to it.

Every year, an elderly German man named Kondau also goes to this celebration with his family. He comes from far away. Anyone would say: "What came over him, that in his right mind he would set out from Germany for such a long trip?"

During the period of the Nazi Occupation, this man was an officer in the German army, and for a time he happened to be the commander of Philiatra. At that time—we are in 1944—some Greek partisans performed some kind of sabotage, killing quite a few Germans in an ambush. The occupiers then became enraged, and the command was given to Kondau from the head-

---

[60] The Holy Hieromartyr St. Charalambos was from Magnesia in Thessaly, Greece, and was martyred under the reign of Emperor Severus in the early third century A.D. at the advanced age of 113. His feast day is celebrated on February 10th.—*Ed.*

quarters in Tripoli to burn half of Philiatra and to execute about a hundred residents on the day that was
about to dawn, at six in the morning.

As was natural, terror and panic overcame all the
inhabitants. They knew that the German commands
were irrevocable. Nothing could save them from destruction and calamity. In the morning (July 19th) however, although the appointed time came, they didn't
see any movement. They wondered, what in the world
had happened?

That night, the faithful had sought Saint Charalambos' protection with burning tears, and he took
action miraculously. He appeared to the German commander, Kondau, and told him to not execute the command. He furthermore promised him that he would
not be punished by his superior, and that he and his
soldiers would return safely to their homeland.

In the beginning, Kondau seemed cold and unmoved. Altogether, the Saint appeared to him three
times to convince him that this was something supernatural and that he had to obey. The admirable thing
is that the Saint also appeared to the German general
in Tripoli.

That morning, Kondau asked for the priests of the

four parishes of the city. They appeared terrified before him. How could they know what had intervened that night! Together with them, he went around to the churches of Philiatra and observed the icons.

In the fourth church, the Entrance of the Theotokos, the so-called '*Gouviotissa*', seeing an icon—an elderly man with a very white beard, dressed in priestly vestments—he shouted: "There! That's him!" and fell down before him to venerate him. As soon as he got up he told the surprised priests: "You were saved by this saint, who also saved me from a grave crime."

Thus, by the intervention of its patron saint, the city escaped from fire and slaughter. A very vivid and moving miracle. The souls of all the Christians were steeped in deep emotion.

In 1945, when the war had already ended, the officials of Philiatra were notified by Kondau to expect him also for the Saint's celebration. He would be coming with his family to thank the Saint, who, as he promised him, had returned him to his homeland safe and sound. Indeed, due to car trouble and some other obstacles, he happened to arrive on February 12th.

The people of Philiatra and all the inhabitants of the area had prepared an enthusiastic reception for him. For his sake they repeated the celebration. He went up onto a balcony and spoke to the crowd in Greek. Moreover, he told them that before departing for Greece he saw Saint Charalambos in his sleep again, and he told him: "I'm waiting for you in Philiatra, where you demonstrated your faith. Everyone will welcome you with great joy." Emotion and sacred enthusiasm overcame all of them.

And the local registry of saints notes: "On this day, the nineteenth of July, we celebrate the memory of the excellent miracle of the holy glorious Hieromartyr Charalmbos, by whose intercessions to God many of the citizens of Eranis were saved from a sure death sentence under the German occupying forces in the year 1944."

Truly "wondrous is God in his saints."

✵ ✵ ✵

Now let's deal with some miracles that have a poetic and Edenic tone, gathering wonders that have to do with flowers.[61]

---

[61] The word 'gathering' used here is one of the meanings of the word *ανθολογώντας*, or 'anthologizing', which is used in the original Greek, and whose root comes from *άνθος*, or 'flower'. Thus Fr. Daniel engages in a clever bit of wordplay.—*Ed.*

The faithful are accustomed to decorating the icons of saints whom they are celebrating with myrtle, laurel, roses, carnations, violets, lilies and other flowers. These are representatives of the plant kingdom which come to concelebrate with the Christians. Sometimes the grace of God—which is manifested more vividly on feast days—falls upon the flowers, alters the laws of biology, and offers some beautiful and charming miracles to the eyes of those who love the festivals.

We'll begin in Cephalonia. Between the villages of Trogianata and Demoutsanata, near Argostoli, there is a chapel called the "Panagia with the Little Lilies." From the feast of the Annunciation, they place vases with lilies in front of the icon of the Theotokos, which, as is natural, dry up after a few hours. They don't disturb them, however. Although more than four months pass and August 15th comes, in an exceedingly wondrous manner the stems become green and the lilies blossom, despite the fact that the lower part of the branch remains dry.

And in another of Cephalonia's villages, Pastra, which is located on the southeastern part of the island, the same miracle occurs. In the courtyard of the

Church of the Dormition they plant lilies. When they blossom in May they cut them, form them into bundles, and place them before the icon of the Panagia. They dry up, but from August 1st, when the supplicatory canons of the Theotokos begin, until August 15th, they come to life and bud. After the Divine Liturgy of the feast of the Dormition, the priest distributes them to the Christians as a blessing.

In olden times, the icon was located in the small neighboring village of Upper Valtes, where the same miracle would occur. The local tradition in Valtes says that the icon of the Dormition was found three hundred years ago on the bush-filled heights of Gravala, at the edge of a spring, among white lilies. A shepherd girl discovered it, led by a nanny goat that would go and drink water at that spring, and whose whole body would appear wet. Certain times, when Christians with fervent faith perform a supplication service before the icon of the Panagia, the dry stems of the lilies bloom again for as long as the prayer lasts!

The same miracle is also observed in the Dodecanese Islands, on Leipsi, an island that lies east of Patmos and north of Leros. There, in a church of the Panagia, there is a prototypical icon: the Theotokos holds Christ not as an infant, but as one nailed to the Cross. The people call this icon the "Panagia of Death."

In April of 1943, a certain pious girl cut white lilies and placed them on this icon. After a few days, the lilies dried up. Weeks and months passed. In an amazing manner, the dried lilies began to produce new shoots here and there, especially in July; and on August 23rd—the Ninth Day[62] (that's when the church celebrates)—they opened up as perfect lilies. And those of August were alike in every way to the ones from April.

From 1943 on, the miracle is repeated every year. A resident of Leipsi wrote to me: "In April we place lilies on the icon. As is natural, the lilies dry up completely, and totally mysteriously in July they start putting out buds, which blossom into perfect lilies on the Ninth Day from the Dormition of the Panagia. That day is a gospel of joy for us Leipsiotes."

But something similar also happens in the Cycladic Islands, on Andros, in the village of Apoikia—there, where the famous spring of Sariza is found.

The girls and women of Apoikia cultivate the lilies

---

[62] This is a reference to the Leave-Taking of the Feast of the Dormition of the Theotokos, which takes place on the ninth day from the date of the Dormition feast, and is celebrated with equal pomp and reverence as the Dormition itself in many places in Greece.—*Ed.*

of the Virgin—the "holy lilies of the Panagia," as they call them. When they take care of them, they are always careful to be clean. They place them in an appropriate place. They water them with clean water and holy water. If they don't pay attention to these things, the miracle that we will talk about further below doesn't happen. They flower in the month of May— "May lilies." They produce some thin little lilies that have a sweet smell and symbolize the spotless and fragrant purity of the Ever-Virgin.

The second parish in the village is the famous Panagia "Katasyrti" (the name is due to a miraculous relocation and preservation of the church). When the virginal lilies bloom, they cut branches and place them on the large and ancient miraculous icon of the Panagia that is in that church. After a little while they die, as is natural. They wither, the leaves curl up, and a thin, weak, completely dry stalk remains, which breaks apart if anyone touches it.

As soon as the period of the fifteenth of August[63] approaches, however, little by little the dead plants begin coming to life. And on August 15th, when the

---

[63] Namely, the fifteen day Dormition Fast.—*Ed.*

church celebrates, they are at the peak of their bloom. They have been rejuvenated and have sprouted; they have put out some little buds like very refreshing daisies, and many times they also produce green leaves.

Another amazing thing—the way in which the revived lilies stand in the middle of the glass of the icon is paradoxical. They look like they are floating in mid-air. They ignore the laws of physics. The most wondrous thing, however, is that they are preserved in this flowering state until the spring of the following year, when they usually renew them by replacing them with new cuttings. When they take them from the icon, they are vital and fresh—living patterns of some future resurrection.

These holy lilies present similar displays even if they are placed on icons at other churches—at the Nativity of the Theotokos, further up from Sariza, and at the Monastery of St. Nicholas, above the village. At certain times these blessed lilies also send messages to the Christians. For example, in August of 1940 they did not bloom, and the Christians understood that something bad was coming. Two months later, Italy declared war against our homeland.

The event that also took place in the village of

Polyplatano, near Naousa, is similar. They had framed an icon with flowers of different kinds in a chapel that was celebrating. Of course the flowers dried up, but they remained in their place and still crowned the icon. After a while, however, two or three roses overcame the withering and germinated back to life. As soon as the miracle became known, everyone ran to the chapel full of curiosity. An acquaintance related that something similar had happened in a village of Karditsa, in a crown of flowers that had been placed on the head of an icon of Saint Nicholas.

In the county of Ierapetra,[64] in Crete, in the village of Stavros,[65] or Kapistri, they place dry flowers from the '*epitaphios*'[66] on the icon of Saint John the Theologian. This happens in the chapel of the Saint on the day of his feast (May 8th). During the Divine Liturgy, at the time of the Gospel reading, many of these flowers come back to life. As a Cretan expressed it to me:

---

[64] The name literally means "Sacred Stone."—*Ed.*

[65] As is not unusual in a country such as Greece, with a history spanning many thousands of years, the village apparently has two names. The first name literally means "Cross," while the second name may be an historical carryover from the period of Ottoman rule, or from earlier pre-Christian times.—*Ed.*

[66] The *epitaphios* (ἐπιτάφιος in Greek) is an elaborately embroidered cloth icon representing the burial of Christ, which is processed with great solemnity in a candlelight vigil on Holy Friday.—*Ed.*

"Many of them become fresh." Furthermore, many Christians from Ierapetra set out every year for Stavros on the Saint's feast day, to behold this extraordinary phenomenon.

There are cases in which flowers that crown the Crucified One from the evening of Holy Thursday come back to life. Such miracles resound in accompaniment with the paschal songs of our Church, and with the "I await the resurrection of the dead."[67]

✢ ✢ ✢

When the facts speak so intensely, words and comments are superfluous. And from a little flame that was flickering, faith is transformed into a huge fire that casts out the icy darkness. From an obscure little boat that was traversing the shallows, it becomes an enormous ship that puts out into wide seas.

The wondrous and well-appointed laws of nature, the miraculous interventions of the saints, the bush of Sinai, the catfish of the Jordan, and the little lilies of Cephalonia and of Andros strengthen the anemic and enliven the atrophied. And the weak little tree becomes a mighty oak—the queen of the forest; and the

---

[67] From the Orthodox 'Symbol of Faith', or Nicene Creed.—*Ed.*

roots go deeper and become stronger, so as to face the menaces of the various winds—incredulity, skepticism, doubt, cowardice, and unbelief—victoriously. And then the words of the poet are timely:

> *"Fear not for the tree that stretches*
> *its roots deep into the ground,*
> *even if the wind breaks its crown*
> *and still yet its thickest of branches."*[68]

---

[68] From the poem "In Faith Above, Hope" (*Στην πίστη πάνω, την ελπίδα*) by Greek poet and playwright Ioannis Polemis (1862-1924).—*Ed.*

THIRD HOMILY
(OR "FIVE STONES FROM THE BROOK")

According to the biblical narrative, a thousand years before Christ, the Philistine giant, Goliath—"a mighty man...his height was four cubits and a span"[69]—threatened the Israelites. A little shepherd boy, David, came out to face this frightful man with his staff, his sling, and five round stones he had chosen from a brook as his only weapons. Today there are other kinds of Goliaths that threaten the people of God—the Goliath of heresy, the Goliath of immorality, the Goliath of unbelief, etc.

Let's note the last one, unbelief, and let's attack it like David. As he "chose for himself five smooth stones out of the brook,"[70] so let us also choose five stones, not from some brook of Palestine, but from the realms of science, nature, creation, history, and the Church.

1) *The Bat and Radar.* The Goliath of unbelief battles

---

[69] 1 Kg 17:4—*Ed.*
[70] 1 Kg 17:20—*Ed.*

the idea that behind creation is hidden a supreme Mind—an all wise Creator, who "in wisdom...made them all."[71] Common sense, however, assures us that things are different from what unbelief and atheism profess.

Everyone understands that even for a nail clipper to be made, a mind has to be at work—a mind that conceives of it, a mind that designs it, and a mind that builds it in its technical workshop. Woe be it for someone to say that it came out of nothing, by luck, by coincidence—that it sprang up on its own in front of us.

If this is true for a nail cutter, what then can we say about other complicated and wondrous devices, which, in order to come to light, consumed so much grey matter from innumerable scientists of innumerable generations? One of these devices is radar (from the initial letters of the words **Ra**dio **D**etection **a**nd **R**anging)—an invention that was made just a few years before the Second World War. Its chief inventor is considered to be the Brit, Robert Watson-Watt,[72] even

---

[71] Ps 103:25—*Ed.*

[72] Watt did his first experiment in 1935 from inside a truck stopped along a country road, locating an airplane at a distance of greater than 10 kilometers (6.2 miles). [Sir Robert Alexander Watson-Watt (1892–1973)

though others, like the Italian, Marconi, had paved the way.

It is an admirable apparatus that—with its transmitter, its receiver, its very short pulses of very high frequency electromagnetic energy and the reflection of those pulses—determines the presence of objects which are located at long distances. It is an invention which marked a revolution, which solved unsolved problems, which turned night into day, which has been most useful apart from war—in sailing, in coastal navigation, in flight, and even in astronautics and astronomy—an invention which honors human science. Think then how foolish it would be for someone to show up and maintain that this wondrous apparatus sprang up on its own like a mushroom, without a human mind working on it.

Now let's go to the world of animals, to the class of mammals and the order of *chiroptera*—to the bats—in order to observe a phenomenon there that provokes astonishment.

While their sight is feeble, they can and do move easily and very quickly in the darkness. They fly in

received a patent for his radio device to detect and locate aircraft in April of 1935.—*Ed.*]

deep night and catch numerous insects without ever bumping into wires or branches or columns or walls. Moreover, there are large caves where innumerable ones live, move, fly, and come and go without crashing into each other. Even if someone closes or takes out their eyes (related experiments have been done—the first of which was the experimentation of the Italian, Spallanzani,[73] about 160 years ago), they still move with the same ease in the darkness.

What in the world is happening in these cases? Something wondrous and amazing! The bat is equipped with an apparatus that functions like radar.

In radar we have electromagnetics, whereas here we have ultrasonic waves. From its larynx, which is bony and compact, with many strong muscles, some kinds of signal clicks and cries, which are ultrasonic waves, are emitted. Under amplification, these clicks resemble the "click" we make with our tongue. That's why they are called thus.

These transmissions are brief and pulsed. Twenty

---

[73] Lazzaro Spallanzani (1729-1799) was a Roman Catholic priest, biologist and physiologist, whose early research in microbiology and biogenesis is thought to have laid the groundwork for later European scientists, such as Louis Pasteur. Among his many fields of study was the biology of echolocation. His experiments would actually have taken place more than 200 years from the time of Fr. Daniel's writing —*Ed.*

or thirty may take place per second, according to the type of bat. When the bat is at rest, they decrease to five or ten. When it is flying in an area with many obstacles, they reach fifty. When it is struggling to capture its prey, they become much more frequent.

These ultrasonic waves go outward from the nose, and when they strike any object, they bounce back—a reflection of sound—and are captured by the receivers that are in its ears and which are like a radio's. Thus it imparts the precious information that is so necessary to it to the brain.

That the receivers are located in the ears is certain. It has been observed that when they are blocked up, it immediately loses its orientation and bumps into things here and there. In order not to hear its voice at the moment it is transmitting, it makes use of a pair of acoustic muscles that contract and block its ears.[74] Immediately after the transmissions, the muscles relax and it can again hear the reflection of the sound that interests it.

So ultrasonic waves are transmitted from the larynx. They are conducted outward from the nose. They are reflected, they return, they are captured by the ears and are directed to the brain. In other words, a perfect radar system! Its perfection is so amazing that the naturalists have not yet managed to search out all of its secrets—and constructed on such an inconceivably small scale!

A French scientist, Jean Montorsier, notes:

"All this history presupposes a series of mechanisms (transmission of "clicks," a system of receipt by the ears) whose complexity and precision causes amazement; above all, in whatever regards the brain, where the mechanism of analysis of ultrasonic waves is infinitely more perfect than in our best radar. The signals of the

---

[74] Although largely inaudible to the human ear, at as much as 130 decibels, a bat's own vocalizations could easily deafen it without the kind of protection afforded by these specialized muscles.—*Ed.*

bat, for example, much quicker than our own, travel 30 kilometers, while our own travel just 3.4 kilometers in the same period of time. Moreover—and this point in particular has stunned electrical engineers and "cybernetics" specialists—the extreme microscopic dimensions of this analytical apparatus does not allow for any comparison at all with our own radar."[75]

Here is another amazing phenomenon: there are enormous caves where millions of bats live, and despite this each one distinguishes its own ultrasonic transmissions—it has its own "wavelength"—and its own radar never gets mixed up with the others!

One loses his mind gazing at these astonishing phenomena, and is completely filled with wonder. What wisdom! What majesty! And then the materialists and the atheists come and tell you that these constructs, these amazing masterpieces of skill, of subtlety, of precision, of wisdom, happened by themselves, without some supreme Mind being at work!

2) *The Preparation of Bread without Leaven.* The second

---

[75] This is a loose translation based on Fr. Daniel's own Greek text. The original quote in French, to which the translators did not have access, presumably comes from Montorsier's *Les Bêtes Nos Amies*, Paris: A. Bonne, 1963.—*Ed.*

stone with which we will strike the Goliath of unbelief is related to the chemical phenomenon which is called fermentation. We will therefore first have to say a few words about leaven and bacteria.

Bacteria, which are also called bacilli, comprise single-celled plant organisms, microbes. (It has prevailed for all microorganisms without exception, both plant and animal, to be called microbes. The word bacteria is only for plants. In ancient Greek, a cane, or walking stick, was called *"bacteria."* Because the first ones to be observed resembled small rods, they were thus "baptized.") We encounter them in the air, in the water, in the ground, on the bodies of animals, on plants and in substances coming from plants. They are so small that sometimes they can't even be seen with a microscope. 250,000 can fit in an area equal to that of a period!

Some are harmful to man—"pathogens"—because they produce toxins which poison the human organism, causing various illnesses like the plague, typhus, dysentery, diphtheria, etc. Others are beneficial and very useful. To the second category belong those that convert a dead organic substance to dissolved inorganic components, which comprise the food of chlorophyll-containing plants and, through these plants, of other heterotrophic organisms. Their significance is of the utmost importance in the economy of nature.

The bacteria that secrete leaven are also very beneficial. The exceptionally complex chemical phenomenon called fermentation is caused by this. These microorganisms comprise a tireless army of workers that labor ceaselessly and offer invaluable services.

If not for the phenomenon of fermentation, precious and very necessary types of nourishment would be unknown to us. Bread, cheese, butter, yoghurt, vinegar, wine, beer—all these are products of fermentation. Even alcohol, glycerin, various antibiotics (chrysomycin, penicillin, streptomycin) come from fermentation. Likewise, the working of leather is accomplished through fermentation.[76] According to its activity, fermentation is characterized as lactic, butyric, alcoholic, citric, oxic, etc.

Let's focus on the preparation of bread. Flour, water and salt are not sufficient. Leaven (yeast) is also

---

[76] The manufacture of leather from animal skins requires a number of complex steps, some of which are accomplished through the use of various enzymes. One important class of these, the *proteases*, is obtained as a byproduct of microbial fermentation.—*Ed.*

needed. This creates the fermentation and causes the dough to swell, to puff up, and to rise. Specifically, the rising is due to a gas which is produced during the relevant chemical reactions. In other words, the "kneading" admixture of the leaven breaks down and converts the sugar in the bread dough into alcohol and carbon dioxide. The carbon dioxide trying to escape creates this "rising," or swelling.

But, as we said, in order for the leaven to be produced, the unseen microorganisms called bacteria are needed. If they were absent, we would have neither leaven, nor dough, nor bread that "strengthens man's heart."[77] That is the process. That is the natural order of the thing.

But aside from what is natural there also exists what is beyond nature. And there is the possibility for us to prepare bread in a supernatural way, without bacteria and without leaven. Can something like this happen? Of course! How does it happen? Ask pious Christian women. They know many ways—religious ways. Let's mention one.

They get the flour, the water and the salt ready;

---

[77] Ps 103:15—*Ed.*

they mix them together, they knead them, they cover them, but they do not add leaven. However, on top of it they place a flower from the cross and basil that they got from church on the feast of the Elevation of the Cross. Then they say a prayer, they make the sign of the cross over it—some women have a habit of reading the Epistle passage about the old and new leaven (1 Corinthians, chapter 5)—and they leave it.

After a few hours—something wondrous and mysterious!—the dough has been leavened, has risen, and is ready for the oven. An amazing miracle—a wonderful miracle that has been happening for centuries now with pious Christian women.

"I was hearing about other women," a good Christian woman told me, "leavening that way, and I tried it, too. For so many years I had never decided to do it. I got basil from the priest on the day of the Cross—September 14th—and in the afternoon I started to warm up some water. I threw in the basil, and after the water warmed up a little, I took it out.

"With this water, I put in flour and I let it thicken a little—not much. It became like a little *prosphora*.[78] I

---

[78] Specially prepared bread given as an offering to the Church and used by the priest to prepare the holy Eucharist during the Divine Liturgy.—*Ed.*

crossed it and put the basil on top of it crosswise. I covered it and placed it on a table near the icons, and I prayed. I felt moved. I said, 'I am not worthy to do something like this.'

"Every so often I would go look at it. I had become anxious. But the next morning I was filled with joy, because it had risen and had burst. It was perfect leaven. Afterwards I added more flour. I mixed it up and left it. It also rose. Subsequently I made *prosphora* and bread. I keep it and I always use this for leavening."

In certain areas, something different is customary. For instance, in Tithorea of Phthiotidos,[79] on Holy Friday they mix water with flour, without leavening, and they make a "porridge," which they put in a pan underneath the *kouvouklion* of the *Epitaphios*.[80] At the time the Epistle is read—*"Do you not know that a little leaven leavens the whole lump? Therefore purge out the old leaven..."* (1 Co 5:6-8)—it is miraculously leavened and rises. At the end of the service, the Christian women take a portion.

In other places on the same day, they hold a little

---

[79] An eastern province of the south-central Greek mainland.—*Ed.*

[80] For an explanation of the terms *kouvouklion* and *Epitaphios*, see notes 17 (p. 30) and 66 (p. 82), respectively.—*Ed.*

cup in their hands with flour mixed with water. At the time of the Epistle, they stir it up a little with their hands and it becomes a perfect leavening.

In all these cases, it is customary for the first bread that is prepared to be *prosphora* for the Divine Liturgy. I remember years ago (May 8, 1979) on the feast of Saint John the Theologian, a pious Christian woman brought to the church a very beautiful *prosphora*. "Father," she told me, "use this one in the liturgy. I made it without leaven, with a flower from the cross."

We are dealing here with an exceptional miracle. Furthermore, whoever knows a little about chemistry and enzymology understands better than anyone else how great this miracle is.

But there is also another supernatural event connected with the basil from the feast of the Cross, which offers a sacred joy to the Christian women who behold it. Before it dries up, they place the little sprig of basil they got from the church in a glass or in a vase. They also put in some water. Hours later the miracle begins.

That is to say, the sprig produces small roots on the lower part, which over time increase and multiply. Following that, the good Christian woman puts it in a flowerpot so that it develops into an authentic and bushy basil plant with numerous branches. This beautiful miracle only happens with basil from the Cross. If other basil is used, it does not take place.

Coming back to the leavening, this miraculous leavening can also happen with other sanctified materials. An abbess of a monastery on Aegina—specifically, that of St. Menas—related to me that she leavened *prosphora* for the Divine Liturgy with myrrh from the Panagia Malevi. (We will say a word about this myrrh in the fourth homily.) Likewise, at the monastery of St. David, near the Lake of Euboea, they mentioned to us on one of our pilgrimage excursions that many Christian women leaven with holy water from the spring of Saint David.

3) *The Miraculous Panormitis of Symi.* Now the evil of unbelief will be struck by an archangelic hand. Northwest of Rhodes, sixteen miles away—about two and a half hours by boat—lies a small paradise of the Aegean: the beautiful island of Symi, that is, with its many gulfs, bays, ports and capes. A healthy climate. A life full of tranquility, serenity and simplicity among kindhearted fishermen and sponge divers. And everywhere

an atmosphere of traditional piety.

To the south of the island, at the innermost point of a picturesque port and built up on the rocks, juts out the historic Monastery of Panormitis—that is, of the Archangel Michael. The miraculous icon of the Archangel is kept there.

The monastery of Panormitis (lower right) and its picturesque port.

The Archangel Michael is considered a father, guide, guardian and protector of the people of Symi. He is their boast, their glory, and their crown—their refuge in all the afflictions the sea causes them and in every difficulty of life. They revere him to the utmost. They have dedicated numerous churches and monasteries to him. They take his name: Michael, Taxiarchis, Panormitis, Paermiotis, Michalia, Michalakena. Furthermore, it goes without saying that the children born after a miracle of his—in accordance with the vow of their parents—take his name.

The Monastery of Panormitis is not only a pilgrimage site for Symi, but for the entire Dodecanese,[81] not to speak of all of Greece. It is the chief pilgrimage site of sailors. All year long, thousands of pilgrims arrive there, while on the annual celebration of the Supreme Commander[82]—November 8th—the place gets turned upside down: innumerable pilgrims, ships of all kinds, dedications, emotions, doxologies, prayers. Moreover, on this day you would say that his icon comes alive. His face perspires, and they gather the sweat as a blessing.

Everyone runs with soul aflame to honor the One of Great Grace—so they call him—to beseech him, to thank him and to cry out: "You are great, my *Paermioti!*" For all these people the Arch-General is not an angel of death who brandishes his terrible sword, but the archangel of life.

They even go so far as to sing him some of his charming couplets:

---

[81] The Dodecanese Islands are twelve large islands, as well as their innumerable smaller dependent islets, in the southeastern Aegean.—*Ed.*

[82] According to the Holy Tradition of the Orthodox Church, the Archangel Michael is the commander in chief of the heavenly armies.—*Ed.*

"See me take a dip forty nights in the sea,

　　My good little Paermiotis, and go to your liturgy."[83]

"And of the twelve islands, Symi is in first place,

　　because it has the Holy Paermiotis in its embrace."

"Paermiotis and Christ upon your wreaths,[84]

　　and your hearts' desire may the Panagia bequeath."

"To Paermiotis, a candle and oil everyone offers,

　　and I offer my youth, which the others don't proffer."

There is no way to number the miracles that the Archangel has been performing for centuries now. Anyone who casts an eye on the innumerable votive offerings which hang on his gold- and silver-plated icon and on the "museum of offerings," and thinks about how all of these are related to miracles, will get some kind of an idea. We should also note that quite a few Italians who happen to have become acquainted with the grace of the Panormitis (as it is known, the Italian rule of the island lasted until the end of World War II) take refuge in him and receive his supernatural help.

---

[83] A reference to the forty consecutive daily divine liturgies Orthodox Christians sometimes attend as a special act of piety.—*Ed.*

[84] A reference to the crowns worn by the bride and groom in the Orthodox Christian wedding ceremony.—*Ed.*

The miraculous icon of the Panormitis (Archangel Michael).

Aside from the usual miracles, the Panormitis also performs a completely peculiar and astonishing one. That is, if sailors who are located in the middle of the sea call upon him at some difficult and dangerous hour, they go on to the following strange action. They put wax, incense, olive oil, money, paper with names, and votive offerings into a wooden box; they close it well, they approach the edge of the ship, and with prayers and psalmody—"*Supreme Commander of the heavenly armies...*"[85]—and religious compunction, they throw it overboard, in order for the sea to take it and guide it to the Monastery of Panormitis.

After a few days or weeks they get the reply: "We received your offering. We prayed for you. May the prayers of the Archangel always be with you." Or: "We received your offering—that is, the three apples, the candle, the frankincense, the incense, the oil and the silver eyes.[86] May the prayers of the Archangel be with you."

Speaking with sailors, one learns a lot about the curious voyage to Panormitis. We[87] recently became acquainted with a certain retired ship captain and,

---

[85] From the *apolytikion* of the Synaxis of the Holy Archangels.—*Ed.*

[86] It is common for pious Christians in Greece to dedicate silver-plated votive offerings in the shape of various afflicted body parts as adornments for miraculous icons. The "silver eyes" would be an example of this.—*Ed.*

[87] As is not uncommon in Greek expository writing, Fr. Daniel often uses "we" instead of "I" throughout the text. Most of those references have been converted to the first person, in keeping with English syntactical norms; on certain occasions however, such as the one recounted here, he was most likely accompanied by one or more of his spiritual children, and the third person form has been retained.—*Ed.*

striking up a conversation, he told us the following:

"In 1947, I was traveling with Empeirikos's[88] cargo ship, 'Argolikos', as a lieutenant. We left Alexandria behind us and were headed towards Constantinople, where we would be taking on ore for America. Passing by Rhodes, the Symian helmsman of the ship says to me: 'Captain, there far in the distance is Symi with the Panormitis. If we throw a bottle into the sea, it'll go there on its own.'

"I adopted his suggestion and, together with the captain, we put in names, addresses, a letter, and ten dollars. We sealed it up well and threw it into the water. Two weeks later, my wife in Athens received a letter from the monastery. As to how the dispatch arrived at its destination, the following was written: 'A boatman was sailing a little distance from the monastery. He saw the bottle headed towards here. He thought that some pious people must have thrown it in from afar. He leaned over, got it and turned it over to us.'

"If a Symian neighbor of hers had not been there, she would not have been able to understand anything about

---

[88] Leonidas Andreas Empeirikos (1872-1947) was a shipping magnate and founder of the Greek National Steamship association. He also served as president of several important shipping unions, as a member of parliament, and in a number of capacities as a government minister.—*Ed.*

the matter. 'Since your husband will be going to Amer-
ica,' the committee of the monastery wrote, among other
things, 'we ask him to send us a typewriter, because we
have need of it.' I found out about the particulars full of
emotion, and I eagerly complied with their request. From
then on, every year I go to his grace. The abbot tells me
smiling that they still have the typewriter, and he shows
it to me.

"One time when I became seriously ill and I even had
to undergo surgery, I saw the Archangel in my sleep. He
visited me to announce the operation's success ahead of
time."

That is to say, that which falls into the sea docks in
an unfathomable, mysterious and miraculous manner
at the port of Panormitis. It is a normal phenomenon
for one to see boxes, small boats with incense, wooden
trunks, bottles of olive oil, etc.—which were sent not
only from the Sea of Crete or the Aegean or the Ionian
or the western Mediterranean, but even from the At-
lantic Ocean—floating in this harbor.

This is the One of Great Grace of Symi! This peculiar miracle has been performed for centuries now.
Moreover, once when the monastery was in need of

construction work, there came to the port of Panormitis—who knows from how far away?—as many wooden
planks as were needed.

This is the Christian faith. And whoever wants to
reinforce it even more, let him try taking a trip to
Symi. That way he will verify in person "the certainty
of the word."[89]

4) <u>*September 10, 1943, in Orchomenos.*</u> The fourth stone
we will sling against the Goliath of unbelief is an exceptional miracle that is associated with Orchomenos
of Voiotia. This city is located in the district of Leiv-
adia.

Every year on September 10th, a great feast and
celebration takes place in Orchomenos, with an unheard of gathering of people. If one looks at the calendar, he will not find any holiday that justifies such
festivities. Furthermore, their both large and historic
church is dedicated to the Dormition of the Theotokos.[90] On asking, however, he will learn that on that
day during the German occupation, the Panagia—the
patron saint and protector of the city—performed a

---

[89] From the *Apolytikion* of Holy Theophany (Tone 1).—*Ed.*
[90] The point is that this holiday is celebrated on the 15th of August.—*Ed.*

How the Panagia immobilized the German tanks at Orchomenos.

great miracle. She intervened personally and saved them from certain catastrophe.

It was the beginning of September of 1943. The conquerors were informed that the residents of Orchomenos were responsible for certain anti-German activities—a slanderous fabrication—and they decided to proceed in harsh retaliation, with burning and slaughter. On the night of September 9th they captured 600 young men. Terror spread its specter throughout the city, and most people, scared, began leaving for the surrounding fields.

On September 10th at nightfall, a German phalanx with soldiers and tanks was entering the city. Across from them, not far away, could be seen the Church of the Dormition—the ancient monastery of "Skripous." Some person appeared to come out from there, and behold! In a little while they saw a majestic woman, three meters[91] above the earth, looking first towards the city and crying loudly: "My children, I've lost you tonight!"

The cry was very loud and was heard at a very great distance. The inhabitants of Orchomenos speak of a loud "shouting." And then she turned towards the German phalanx. A powerful flash shot out from her body. The consequences were amazing. The tanks became immobilized in the middle of the road. It was

---

[91] About ten feet.—*Ed.*

completely impossible for them to advance. The next day, in order to pull them into the fields, they had to use a tractor with chains.

Fear and trembling and shock seized the Germans. It didn't take them long to realize that this was something supernatural. Their dispositions changed. Their chief administrator, a tall and imposing man named Hoffmann, gave the order to proceed towards the church in order to venerate the All Holy Virgin. "She saved you," he said. "You must make her silver and glorify her."

In place of rage, now came religious compunction. He immediately commanded that the 600 men who had been captured should be freed. Emotion, awe, religious tremors, and joy overflowed throughout the city. Instead of lamentations, the next day had doxologies, banquets, the roasting of lambs, and a celebration in store.

This is the reason that Orchomenos celebrates every 10th of September. It is worth noting that almost every year Hoffmann comes to the celebration too, bringing other Germans—even up to a whole busload—with him as well. He has also dedicated a large vigil lamp to the church. And in the place where the

Shrine in the place where the Panagia appeared in Orchomenos.

Panagia appeared, a shrine has been erected, where there is now the following inscription (formerly there was another one that was replaced):

THE GREAT MIRACLE OF THE ALL HOLY VIRGIN

TO THE CHAMPION GENERAL AND MOTHER OF GOD, WHO,

BEING A FLOWER FROM HEAVEN PLANTED UPON THE VOIOTIAN

LAND OF SKRIPOUS-PETROMAGOULAS, SAVED IT FROM CER-

TAIN DESTRUCTION AND MASS SLAUGHTER IN THE YEAR OF

SLAVERY AND OCCUPATION 1943, ON THE 9TH OF THE MONTH

OF SEPTEMBER, AT THE TWELFTH HOUR, 12 A.M. MIDNIGHT,

FROM THE VANDALIC GERMAN HORDES.

THIS PILLAR IS PIOUSLY DEDICATED TO HER AS A VERY

SMALL TRIBUTE OF INFINITE GRATITUDE

THE PIOUS RESIDENTS OF SKRIPOUS-PETROMAGOULAS

Every September 10th, an imposing procession occurs from the historic Church of the Dormition to the
shrine. The distance is about six hundred meters.[92]
The metropolitan of the county, a multitude of priests
and thousands of people participate. It is an extremely
moving service.

To whomever doubts these things, Orchomenos is
located neither in America nor in Australia. It is only
129 kilometers[93] from Athens. Let them go and learn
even more things about this wondrous event.

---

[92] About four-tenths of a mile.—*Ed.*
[93] About 80 miles. Fr. Daniel is clearly addressing a Greek audience
here.—*Ed.*

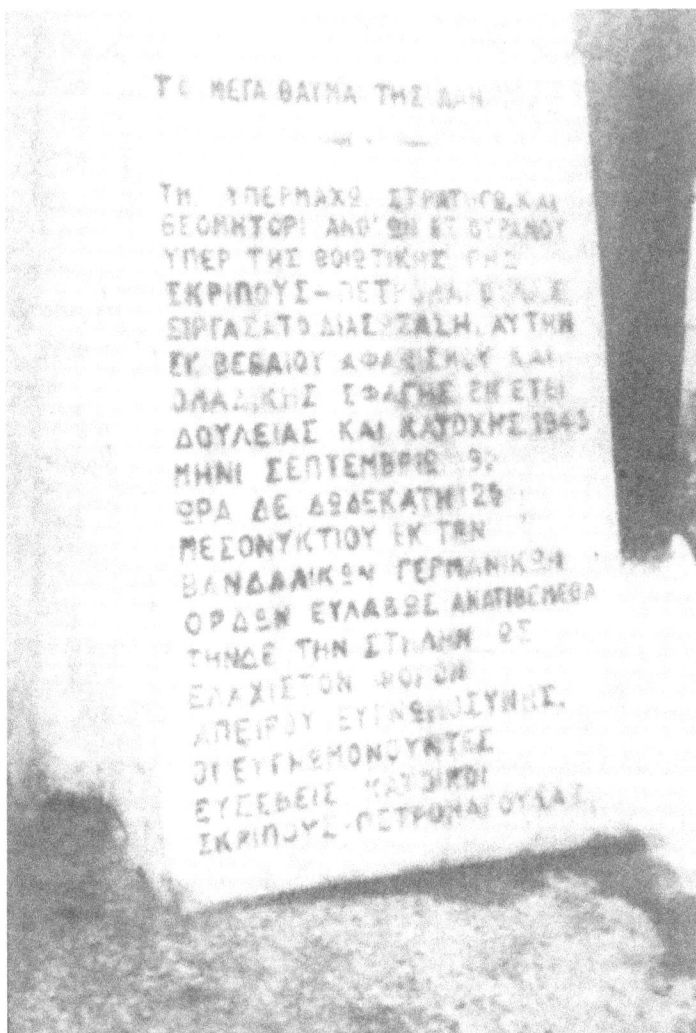

The inscription that describes the miracle.

I remember once when I passed by there, I stopped an elderly gentleman on the road.

—*Is it true*, I asked him, *that the Panagia appeared here and saved you from the Germans?*

As soon as his mind turned towards these events, he felt moved, cried and answered:

—*Ah! I had four children, and the Germans would have slaughtered all four of them on me. But our Panagia saved them....*

5) <u>*The Island That No Longer Has Snakes*</u>. Among the islands of the Aegean there is also the small but glorious island of Psara. (Remember: *"The all-black ridge of Psara...."*)[94] There was a monastery there in olden times in the area called the 'Snake Pit', dedicated to the 'Holy Kioura', that is to Saint Matrona. As even the name shows, snakes were plentiful. Thus one time during a Divine Liturgy, a small snake fell into the Holy Communion. As soon as the priest saw it, he was horrified. What could he do? He couldn't throw it away, because the snake had absorbed Holy Communion. He was forced to eat it![95]

However, he became so indignant and tired in soul

---

[94] The opening line of the poem "The Destruction of Psara" by Greek national poet Dionysios Solomos, in which he describes the island's final devastation during the War of Independence of 1821. The "Black Ridge" was the name of the island's main fortress, which was blown up by the defenders as it was being stormed by thousands of Turkish troops.—*Ed.*

[95] According to ecclesiastical tradition and liturgical rubrics, the celebrating priest must consume anything that remains in the Holy Chalice after the completion of the Divine Liturgy.—*Ed.*

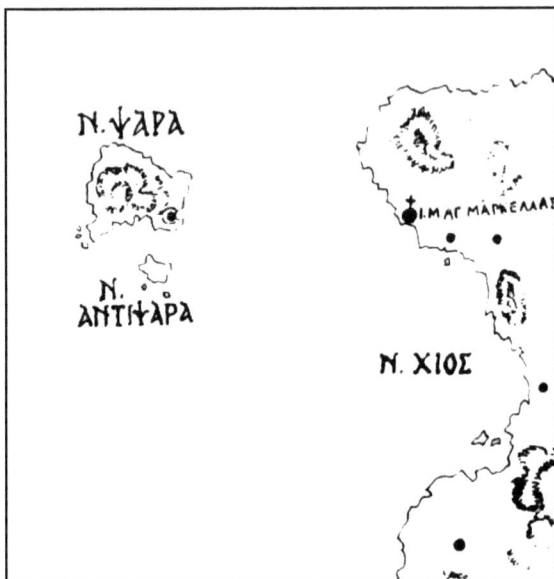

Map of Psara, about 14 miles from Chios.
There are no snakes on the island.

that he entreated God with a loud cry to wipe the snakes out from the island. He cursed them all to disappear; and the result was that, from that moment until today, not even one snake exists on Psara. Incredible but true! Many times snakes have been brought from neighboring islands as a test, and as soon as they advanced three or four meters[96] onto the beach, they died.

I recall, years ago in a sermon in the village of Upper Oropos in Attica, I mentioned the said instance. At

---

[96] Ten or thirteen feet.—*Ed.*

the end a listener approached me. "I'm a teacher," he tells me, "and I also served on Psara for ten years. It's exactly as you said it. Moreover, I can add that if we transport dirt from the 'Snake Pit' to other areas, it saves them from snakes." That good teacher also provided me with the book, *Folklore of Psara*, from which we copy the following lines:

> *"If by chance snakes are transferred in the cavities of trees that the waves cast up onto Psara, they cannot live, but they die as soon as they disembark onto dry land.... Many strangers who visit Psara take dirt from the aforementioned chapel, the 'Snake Pit', and they transport it to other parts of Greece, where strangely the snakes vanish from the homes in which they place it or scatter it. The writer of these lines also confirmed this. Ever since he placed the 'snake dirt' in the four corners of his paternal home, no snakes appeared. When, later on, repairs were done and the 'snake dirt' was scattered, the snakes began appearing again."*[97]

✦ ✦ ✦

While David was supplied with five stones from the brook, he did not use them all, because the first one

---

[97] Demetrios G. Spanos, *Folklore of Psara*, Athens, 1962, p. 76.

was enough to annihilate the opponent. "And David slung one stone and struck the foreigner on his forehead and he fell upon the ground."[98]

We slung all five stones against the enemy; and we hope that every well-intentioned soul who has read these lines will feel how fake the armor of every Goliath is, and how strong and invincible the stone of faith is. "Alas!" cries the sacred Chrysostom, "how great is the power of faith!"

The exceptional radar of the bat, the wondrous leavening with the flower of the Cross, the miraculous Panormitis of great grace, the astonishing intervention of the Panagia at Orchomenos, the surprising disappearance of snakes from Psara—all of these are sacred stones that strike and knock down the Philistine of atheism and unbelief.

Let us provide these stones to whomever does battle with the most insolent Goliath, and they will put down his fury and his "strengthless audacity." They will crush the "hateful and loathsome head,"[99] and they will throw him down as an "exquisite corpse," so

---

[98] This is a paraphrase of 1 Kg 17:28.—*Ed.*
[99] From the *Iambic Canon of the Holy Theophany* of St. John of Damascus, Ode 3, Second Canon.—*Ed.*

that it becomes understood that there also exists another power, before which the swords and spears of the God-opposing powers pale.

The power of faith—embrace it, all you wretched wayfarers of the earth, and you will feel that from having been sparrows you will become eagles! How enviable it is to spread wide an eagle's wings and traverse the azure skies, and how the horizons open before one's eyes! And what skies—what horizons! They are such that eyes diseased from the myopia of atheism have never seen, nor have they even imagined.

O, my Christ, in your sacred Gospel a certain father of an epileptic child is mentioned, who said a lamentable word to you: "If you can, heal my son." You answered him: "If you can believe...." Make us all able to believe! Only then will we feel spiritual majesties— those things that anyone who has pursued unbelief has not encountered.

O, our Lord! Make the rock of faith increase and grow within us, and become a very high mountain like Olympus, like the Alps, and like the Himalayas, so that our being may be enriched with indomitable strength and might, exquisite nobility, bravery and greatness!

Fourth Homily

Again, a word about faith. Again we will take some walks around the exceedingly wondrous grounds of the Church, in order to take note of situations and events that resemble windows into the supernatural world. Again we will touch the majesty of the super-sensory, the extraordinary, the divine. Again we will see normal causes and natural laws being breached.

We will make a stop in the realm of the saints. We will busy ourselves with things which belong to the saints, which speak about them, and which are related to them. We begin with their portrayal.

The icons of the saints that proclaim the great miracle of faith are numerous. Many of these, which as it shows were rendered by pious people with prayer and fasting, exhibit important divine signs. Some remained untouched in a fire, others gushed myrrh, others shed tears, others emitted a powerful radiance, others moved or even traveled, others bled when they were cut with a knife, others made the bullet turn back when they were shot at, others changed their gaze and their expression, others sent some message or other in a particular manner (for example, a knocking sound), etc. Usually these icons are called miraculous. Let's present some specific circumstances.

On Athos,[100] in the Sacred Monastery of Iveron, there is the Panagia *'Portaitissa'* ('Guardian of the Gate'; they placed it in the church and found it at the gate of the monastery)—a large icon (4'6" x 3'1") and one of a kind. It is considered a palladium and guardian of the whole Holy Mountain. The face of the Panagia holding the Infant stands out with an imposing majesty and austerity. She does not resemble the mother of the sweet Nazarene, but of the impartial Judge.

It is known that in the ninth century it was found in Nicaea of Bithynia, in the possession of a pious widow, who in order to save it from the hands of the iconoclasts threw it into the sea. "Borne upon the waves" in a supernatural manner, it arrived at the monastery of Iveron. Innumerable traditions, oral and written in the Greek, Georgian and Russian languages,

---

[100] Mt. Athos, also known as the 'Holy Mountain', is an autonomous monastic republic within the borders of Greece. It is located on an isolated peninsula in northern Greece, and has been one of the foremost monastic centers of the Orthodox Faith for well over a thousand years.—*Ed.*

Icon of the Panagia 'Portaïtissa' (Mt. Athos).

refer to its wonders.

Not only the icon itself, but even its copies are surrounded by a miraculous splendor. The form of the

icon has a distinctive mark, in that on the right cheek, or rather the jaw, a stab mark and blood can be noticed. On the original, there is a wound with dried blood, having come from the Arab pirate, Rachai—the later Saint Barbarus.

When on the eve of August 15th, the feast of the Dormition, the icon is transferred to the large church, then the vigil lamp in front of the Royal Doors breaks out into a strange festive motion, like a kind of sacred dance, which spreads chills and amazement to the crowded pilgrims. Let it be noted that in certain other instances it makes different movements—and not joyful ones—which forebode calamities. Such movement was also observed in 1974, before the Turks invaded Cyprus.

In 1960, a copy of the icon in America—in Oceanside (Hempstead), Long Island, New York—stirred up the Greek-Americans, as well as those of other ethnicities and the heterodox, with a miraculous flow of tears. It is now known as the Tear-Streaming Panagia of Oceanside. Tears flowed constantly from the Panagia's eyes. Scientists who put them through chemical

Tear-Streaming Icon of the Panagia in Hempstead, New York.

analysis found them to be human.[101]

---

[101] In the spring of 1960, three different paper icons of the Panagia began streaming tears in private homes in the Hempstead, Long Island area. After being examined by then Archbishop Iakovos, they were relocated to St. Paul's Greek Orthodox Church in Hempstead for public veneration. There are a number of contemporary news articles about the phenomena available on the internet, and certain accounts indicate that a 'major' New York newspaper had the tears from the icon to which Fr. Daniel refers tested in a laboratory. These accounts claim that the tests found the tears to have consisted of an unknown "oily substance" that did not correspond to any known elements.—*Ed.*

Litany and Enshrinement of the Sacred Tear-Streaming Icon of the Panagia

The Reverend Archbishop of America, Iakovos, assisted by numerous priestsand carrying the sacred icon of the Tear-Streaming Panagia ('Portaïtissa of Iveron) amidst thends of thousands of Christians from all churches and confessions, on the evening of Holy Thursday, April 14, 1960. They transfered it in a procession from the home of Peter and Antonia Koulis (Oceanside, Long Island, NY), pictured above, to the sacred church of the Holy Apostle Paul in Hempstead, Long Island, NY, where the sacred icon was enshrined.

"Thousands of pilgrims continue to gather daily in the Sacred Church of St. Paul, in Hempstead, Long Island, N.Y. to venerate the miraculous holy icon of the tear-streaming Panagia of Oceanside, and to pray from the depths of their heart before her.

"They are not only Greek Orthodox. Among them are also Orthodox of other nationalities, lay people, clergymen, bishops and metropolitans, Catholics and Protestants, of every class, occupation, ethnicity and age. Not a few of them offer gifts and precious devotions. Others bring their sick for healing. And everyone glorifies God, because in our days, when materialism and rationalism prevails, He has been pleased to show His divine might through the flood of tears of the sacred icon of the Mother of God, which has not stopped streaming tears."[102]

The photographs presented show this exceptional and impressive event in relief.

In the Peloponnese, the monastery of the Panagia

---

[102] *Orthodox Observer*. New York: Greek Orthodox Archdiocese of North and South America, May 1960. [Editor's Note: Since the original article in English was not available to the translators, the excerpt cited above has been rendered into English using Fr. Daniel's Greek translation. It is therefore likely to contain discrepancies from the article's original text.]

Worshippers in Veneration of the Icon at St. Paul's Greek Orthodox Church in Hempstead, Long Island.
Interior of the sacred Church of St. Paul in Hempstead, Long Island, New York. In the spring of 1960, it was floded every day with crowds of Christians from all churches and confessions, who came to piously venerate the icon of the Tear-Streaming Panagia and to pray before it.

of Malevi is built on the northern slope of Mt. Parnon-
as. There a small, ancient silver-clad icon of the Dormition has constantly exuded myrrh since 1964. The
myrrh gushes mysteriously from the upper part of the
icon, and from the two sides like drops of condensa-
tion that constantly flow downwards and make little
rivulets on it. Certain times the flow is so excessive
that it runs over onto the icon stand and the floor. It is
collected with cotton.

The aroma is exceptional in quality, as well as in
duration. Ten years ago, I put a little inside a book of
mine, and the infused pages still have a sweet fragrance. An aroma maker once told me that if we pour
even the strongest fragrances from Paris somewhere,
they evaporate completely after twenty-four or forty-
eight hours at the most.

Likewise, this myrrh is also miraculous. Numerous
sick people with grave and incurable maladies who
were anointed with it, or who crossed the diseased
body part with it, or drank it dissolved in water, found
their cure. In a small book published by the ever-
memorable lay preacher, Demetrios Panagopoulos, I
counted numerous instances of cures from cancer
alone (aside from other afflictions): cancer of the

brain, of the throat, of the breast, of the uterus, of the cheek, of the blood, of the stomach, of the large intestine. All the details of those cured are also presented.

A majestic icon of the Supreme Commander Michael in the town of Mandamados, in the north of Lesbos[103], has great miracle-working abilities. It is a pilgrimage site for all of Lesbos.

This icon is one of a kind. In bas-relief, its face, head, hands, wings and sword can be felt. "It is entirely tangible, having a head and body and hands with a sword and wings, as indeed a most fearsome warrior," notes a text from the beginning of the 17th century.

It is to be found in a large church, to the right as we enter. It has been made with the blood of martyrs—from dirt mixed with the blood of monks slaughtered by pirates or Turks who raided the monastery. One monk escaped the slaughter—he who crafted the icon.

"The sacred icon lies within a luxurious *kouvouklion*,[104] bearing the date March 26, 1766. Only his face shows. In his left hand, covered by the *kouvouklion*, he

---

[103] Greece's third largest island, Lesbos (also known as Mytilini) is situated in the northeastern Aegean sea, and is separated from Turkey by a strait of only 3.5 miles at its narrowest point.—*Ed.*

[104] See note 17 (p. 30) for the meaning of this term.—*Ed.*

bears a parchment with an inscription. Above and around his head is an illustration of our Lord in the midst of the Apostles.[105]

Miraculous icon of the Archangel Michael at Mandamados, Lesbos, Greece.

Some pilgrims he receives with good will, and others with disfavor. In the first case, the Archangel's face is calm and reddish, like a living person's. In the second case, it becomes very black and fearsome and inspires terror. In the years of Turkish rule, the conquerors were afraid of the Archangel and did not come near to molest his church, "the Hagarenes not daring to touch it at all because of the daily miracles."[106]

---

[105] Iakovos of Mithymna, *The Pilgrimage of the Archangel Michael of Mandamados*. Mytilini: 1968, p. 17.

[106] The source of this quotation is unclear; however, it presumably comes from the above-referenced work of Iakovos of Mithymna.—*Ed.*

There are moments when drops of sweat run from his forehead, which they gather with cotton for a blessing. And on the day of his celebration, the characteristics of his face become lively and take on a very vivid expression, as if he wants to tell you: "I am alive—I am present."

To the side of the icon one sees iron shoes. The Christians offer them to him. They get old within six months; in this way, the Archangel shows that he walks around the entire island, wherever they ask for him.

In a large celebration that takes place in the spring (there is another one on the 8th of November, as well), on the second Sunday after Pascha, the famous "couscous"—a food which is basically comprised of beef and wheat—is offered to thousands of pilgrims. The ox is slaughtered after a related service. The amazing thing is that, before it is sacrificed, it goes outside the church by itself and kneels and venerates an icon of the Archangel—something which spreads extreme emotion among the numerous pilgrims.

Another wondrous thing is that many Christians travel kilometers on foot to come to his feast. And it happens in a mysterious manner that they do not feel fatigue from the hours-long walk. Someone gives their feet wings.

The Archangel of Mandamados protects the people of Lesbos in a variety of ways. Indeed the liberation of the island from the Turkish yoke in 1912 took place on November 8th, the day of his grace. On that day, the bells of the churches celebrated a double feast. While the Archangel was being celebrated, divisions of the Hellenic Army were disembarking from the legendary Averof.[107]

Through all of their difficulties, the Christians of Lesbos cry out: "Archangel, save me!" A moving case is reported about a man from Lesbos who worked far from the island as a truck driver in a foreign country and fell asleep at the wheel. As soon as he opened his eyes, he realized that he was plunging over a precipice. Terrified, he cried out: "Archangel, arrive!" And the miracle happened. At the bottom of the cliff the whole truck was pulverized, but nothing happened to him and the cab. As soon as he returned to the island he made an offering of the ox that was to be slaughtered at the feast of the Archangel.

---

[107] The Italian-built *Giorgos Averof* was the flagship of the Royal Hellenic Navy for most of the first half of the twentieth century.—*Ed.*

In the prefecture of Elias, near Amaliada, the Panagia of Phragavilla also exhibits something especially impressive. The expression on her face changes. Sometimes it looks at you seriously, other times with strictness, and still other times with sweetness. And at certain times it sends messages with loud knocks.

Many supernatural and strange things happen with an ancient and large icon at a monastery near Chrysoupoli in Kavala. It is a women's monastery honoring the name of the Transfiguration of the Savior, and it is located in a barren, mountainous area outside of the village of Nikitai.

On August 6th, a multitude of people gather there. After the Divine Liturgy, the people go to an open area above the church. They make a circle around the icon. The following is customary: One by one they proceed towards the icon to embrace it. When they sit down with their legs together and outstretched, and their back straight, they receive it. As if it is a living person that moves, the icon hits some of them hard and pushes them down. It hits them crosswise—first on the sides, then on the head, and finally on the feet—and it makes them frightened and as if they have fainted.

This happens, in my opinion, to remind us of how

the three disciples fell on the ground as soon as they beheld the divine cloud and heard the thunderous voice of the Father at Tabor. "And when the disciples heard it, they fell on their faces and were greatly afraid."[108]

A Christian woman from Kavala, following a related supplication service, wrote to me:

"It does miracles. I saw it with my own eyes. This happens only on the day of the Transfiguration. Whoever wants to hold the icon writes their names... No one knows exactly whom it's going to hit. I held the blessed icon. Because some other woman was afraid, she asked to come with me to hold it. I let her. She was extremely frightened. I wasn't afraid, except that, only when I took it a little, I felt a sacred fear. I began to pray. I said the 'Our Father' and the Creed, and as soon as I finished I stood up. It didn't hit me, nor did it even move for me.

"As soon as I got up, some man took it. Oh—my Christ!—if you had seen him. It threw him down. You would have said that his feet had become unscrewed from his shinbones. And the way it was rolling on him— once to the right, once to the left, and then from his head

---

to his feet. He was constantly holding the icon—he couldn't control it—until it left him almost unconscious. They took it from his hands. They gave him holy water and he recovered... You should see young mothers with babies in their arms, how it threw them down!... I wish that you would go and see it. It happens on the feast day of the Transfiguration according to the new calendar.[109] The army, police guards, seven priests, a bishop and an innumerable gathering of people are there."

However, we will especially dwell on the wondrous manifestations of an icon of Christ the Bridegroom in Athens. In April of 1981, over seven days from the 22nd until the 28th, a simple paper icon of Christ the Bridegroom—Christ sorrowful with the crown of thorns—moved with supernatural trembling at the magisterial courthouse at 6 Anaxagora Street—something that created intense religious emotions and greatly occupied the press, as well as the television networks.

More specifically, on Holy Wednesday, a date dedicated by the Church to the Bridegroom, on the sixth floor of the courthouse, above the desk of the supervisor, a noise was heard as if a large clock were peal-

---

[109] The Gregorian, or civil calendar.—*Ed.*

ing. The time was a quarter to three in the afternoon. The thirty-seven year-old secretary of the court, Mrs. Euthymia Koutsolelou, saw the icon of Christ moving. She thought that there was an earthquake.

She turned towards the electric lamp, but saw that it wasn't moving. She looked at the icon again. It was shaking back and forth, and was hitting the wall— slowly at first, and then more intensely. Frightened, she ran and shouted and stirred up the employees. They all went into the office. Stunned, they saw the wondrous movement.

From 2:45 p.m. until 3:00 p.m., the movement did not stop. A hiatus was noted for a quarter of an hour. In the meantime, men from the emergency services arrived. At 3:15 p.m. it started again more intensely, and lasted until 6:45 p.m. A policeman kept it still with his hand, but as soon as he removed it, the motion continued. As he himself said, "it was lifting itself up two or three centimeters[110] from the wall."

The next day, Holy Thursday, it began moving around ten o'clock in the morning. The thing spread. Priests, judges young and old, and a crowd of people

---

[110] About an inch.—*Ed.*

inundated the courthouse. But neither could the people see it comfortably and venerate it, nor could any work get done in the court. "Move the icon to a church!" the faithful shouted.

The icon of Christ the Bridegroom that moved.

Due to the holidays, the courthouse closed and opened on Easter Tuesday. On Tuesday morning the movement continued. On that day, the following docu-

ment was sent to the supervisor of the court-house by
the Ministry of Justice, since they had come to an
understanding with Archbishop Seraphim:

> *"Following the events of the rhythmical movement*
> *without the influence of human power of an icon of Jesus*
> *Christ, found in the Magisterial Court of Athens, and the*
> *great gathering of people on account of this, resulting in*
> *the obstruction of the work of your Service, we ask that*
> *you hand over the aforesaid icon to the Sacred Church of*
> *St. Constantine of Athens, to which parish the branch of*
> *the Magisterial Court belongs."*

Thus, at noon on the same day, the icon was transferred in a procession to St. Constantine, where it was
placed on a stand and adorned with roses. Immediately a multitude of Christians came to venerate it with
compunction, with emotion, and with flowers. The
press recorded:

> *"Young and old accompanied the Crucified One for*
> *hours. A popular pilgrimage to the icon of Christ.*
> *Mothers bring their paralyzed children to the icon of*
> *Christ expecting a miracle. Women decorate the icono-*
> *stasis with flowers and others sprinkle it with perfumes.*
> *Never before has the Church of St. Constantine in*

Omonoia gathered together so many believers. The number of people who entered the church yesterday to venerate the icon that moves is estimated at 10,000."[111]

And some other wondrous things happened. For instance, on Easter Wednesday, at seven o'clock in the evening, the two chandeliers that were located near the icon began swinging, to the great surprise of the faithful who waited their turn to venerate it. All the next days a gathering of people continued in the church. Even today, after so much time, many people are drawn by this icon of the sorrowful and thorn-bearing Christ, and direct their steps that way.

The last thing we will mention about holy icons also has a "green" cast to it[112], because it is associated with a certain plane tree.

In the Peloponnese, on the road between Aigio and the Great Cave,[113] we find the village Plataniotissa. It is beautifully situated and exceptionally pictur-esque, with many plane trees, next to the river Cery-

---

[111] *The Evening Post* (*Η Βραδυνή*), April 30, 1981.
[112] The phrase in the original Greek is: "a nature-loving color...."—*Ed.*
[113] The Great Cave, high up on the side of a cliff, is the location of an ancient monastery of the same name built directly into the rock face. The wonderworking icon of the Panagia mentioned further on in the text is housed there.—*Ed.*

nitis. Many Christians flock to this village to see a certain sacred imprint in the interior of a huge plane tree.

In 840 A.D., monks from the Great Cave, having the miraculous icon of the Panagia with them, were returning to the monastery. They spent the night at Plataniotissa, and they slept in the hollow of the trunk of a large plane tree, hanging the icon high up near the ceiling. In the morning, as they were preparing to quit the place, they were amazed to discover there—high up on the interior of the tree, exactly across from where the icon was hanging—that a bas-relief imprint of it had been formed, as if it had been stamped with some kind of seal.

This amazing event impressed all the Christians of the area, who immediately transformed the hollow of the plane tree into a chapel, which has been preserved up until our days. It resembles a catacomb. One person can fit in its sanctuary, and twelve to fifteen people can fit in the rest of the space.

Anyone who can, should visit this sacred plane tree and should behold the imprint of the Mother of God. If you have doubts, the sanctified tree calls out to you: "Come and see!"

Church of the Panagia Plataniotissa, inside an ancient plane tree, with the miraculous icon imprinted on the tree's interior.

❈ ❈ ❈

The saints honored and glorified God, and because of this they were glorified by Him in return. We previously saw wondrous and supernatural conditions and manifestations of their icons. Now we will see the divine grace that their holy relics contain.

Some of these have a yellowish shade. During the exhumation of holy persons, the people exclaim: "He became sanctified. Look at his relics—they're as yellow as amber," or "as a lemon." Others also have some rosy, reddish lines. Still others have the famous cross-like seam on the skull; that is, on top of the usual seams, one that passes through the middle of the bone of the forehead and reaches down to the nose, with the result that it forms an enormous cross on the skull.

Others are fragrant—whether constantly, or during feast days, or in fixed or extraordinary circumstances. Now an exceptional fragrance comes to mind, which I perceived when I venerated the holy relics that are kept at the monastery of St. George in Arma, in Euboea, near Phylla of Chalkida.

A Lavriote monk told me about the amazingly intense fragrance that pours out every January 1st, during the procession of the skull of St. Basil the Great, which is kept at the Athonite monastery of the Great Lavra.[114] You would think that they were breaking many bottles of perfume.

An exceptional fragrance is also produced by the recently discovered relics of Hieromartyr Ephraim, martyred by the Turks in 1426 A.D. They are located at the Monastery of the Annunciation of the Theotokos in Nea Makri, Attica. When they were discovered in 1965, their first sign was a fragrant smell. We copy here from a relevant book:

> *"The worker began to dig... Continuing now with the sacred disinterment, and reaching a depth of about 1.7 meters,[115] the spade first brought to light the head of the man of God. At that same moment, an inexpressible fragrance spread throughout all of the surrounding atmosphere."[116]*

But talking about the relics of saints tends to become lengthy. It is a table laden with rich foods. We'll

---

[114] The Great Lavra (*Μεγίστη Λαύρα* in Greek) is the ranking monastery in honor on Mt. Athos, having been founded by St. Athanasios the Athonite in 963 A.D.—*Ed.*

[115] Roughly 5.5 feet.—*Ed.*

[116] *Visions and Miracles of the Holy Great-Martyr and Miracle-Worker Ephraim, the Newly Revealed*, N. Makri: 1982, p. 19. [This is a loose translation based on the original Greek text quoted by Fr. Daniel.—*Ed.*]

leave fragrances alone and go on to incorruption.

The incorrupt relics of saints is one of the most beautiful chapters of Christian hagiology. Here the laws of biology are festively abolished. "Doubtful" thoughts are nullified, and the flower of faith blossoms forth full of freshness and life and light.

I remember, one time I ended up in Kyllini, Elis[117] on the 17th of December. Something was pushing me to head for neighboring Zakynthos, whose patron saint was being celebrated. I headed for the majestic church of St. Dionysios. At the end of the right aisle, his relic was on display for veneration. This time it had been taken out of the casket and set upright. A miracle of God was full of life before me!

While the hierarch had died more than four hundred years before, his body had not succumbed to decomposition and decay. It was incorrupt and undissolved. I was seeing natural laws rendered obsolete here, and at the same time a small representation of the future incorruption of bodies after the general resurrection.

Whereas three years after death is enough to dis-

---

[117] Elis (Ηλείας in Greek) is one of Greece's major regions, located in the western Peloponnese.—*Ed.*

solve bodily integrity and to transform flesh, skin, veins, nerves, etc., to dust, here four hundred whole years had passed without causing decomposition and corruption. And of course this wonder is observed not only with Saint Dionysios—the same thing also happens with the body of Saint Gerasimos, which is located in Cephalonia. He also died more than four hundred years ago—on August 15, 1579, to be exact.

The same thing also occurs with the relics of Saint Christodoulos, who founded the renowned monastery of Patmos. Furthermore, the incorruption here has endured for nine hundred years.

The same thing also happens with Saint Savvas, who died more than one thousand five hundred years ago (in 533 A.D.); moreover, his incorrupt body has been through an adventure. In the thirteenth century A.D., the Crusaders transported it to Venice. But in October of 1965 it was restored to the Patriarchate of Jerusalem. When the airplane made a stopover in Athens, Orthodox clergymen, who were thinking of putting vestments with Orthodox colors on him, received it; but they hesitated, because they imagined it to be wooden and inflexible. However, as soon as the head bishop tried, he felt chills. The hands, the feet, the neck, the head, and the waist were all supple—as if it were a living person! Thus they easily adorned him with the new vestments.

That is to say, apart from the incorruption—the first miracle—flexibility of the limbs was also discovered—a second miracle. Let the emission of an exceptional fragrance from time to time—a third miracle—also be added, as well as the performance of cures for sick people and other signs—a fourth miracle. It should be noted that bodies that are preserved with the help of chemicals—the embalmed—resemble boards. They cannot be moved even one centimeter.[118]

Fifteen centuries ago on Cyprus, a bishop—the most exceptional and virtuous person of the large island—died. Today his body is found on Corfu, incorrupt. Even his eyeballs are preserved! It is miracle-working, with all kinds of miracles, and supple. Certain times, when he is carried around at celebrations, he lifts his bent head up high—something which the people of Corfu take as a good sign that "the Saint is pleased." These are the relics of Saint Spyridon.

Now that we've talked about "a good sign," an old

---

[118] About a half-inch.—*Ed.*

story comes to mind about the right hand of St. John the Baptist, which was to be found in Antioch of Syria for about nine hundred years. About the middle of the tenth century it was translated to the royal capital. The Antiochians experienced many strange things from the hand of the Forerunner. We will note the most impressive.

On September 14th, together with the Cross, they also exalted his precious hand in order to draw to it the thousands of eyes that waited to behold the astonishing sign. If he spread out his fingers, it presaged blessings. If he drew them together, it was a bad omen. *"At times,"* we read in the *Synaxarion*[119] for January 7th, *"he spread out his fingers, and at other times he gathered them together, and with the spreading or gathering he revealed future happiness or misfortune."* A dead hand that moves its fingers and simultaneously predicts the future! "Great is the Lord, and great is his might!"

There are incorrupt bodies of saints above Loutraki (St. Patapios), in Prokopio of Euboea (St. John the Russian), in Kalymnos (the newly revealed St. Savvas), in New Karvali of Kavala (St. Gregory Nazianzen, not

---

[119] A liturgical book of the Orthodox Church containing information about the saints and ecclesiastical events commemorated each day.—*Ed.*

whole), and in Corfu (St. Theodora the Empress—the queen who defended Orthodoxy against the iconoclasts in the 9th century A.D.). There are also numerous relics of saints adorned with incorruption in the Orthodox countries of the north—in Serbia, in Bulgaria, in Romania, and above all in Russia. Furthermore in the *lavra*[120] of the Kiev Caves—there, where a multitude of ascetics were sanctified—more than seventy are preserved! And in the ancient monastery of the city of Pechory in Estonia[121] (200 km south of St. Petersburg) about a hundred are preserved!

For anyone who dwells in Athens and wishes to see a miracle of this type without a great deal of effort, I recommend taking a walk up to Perissos. There in the Church of Saint Eustathios, the body of Hieromartyr George of Neapolis—which the pious refugees brought from Asia Minor—is preserved, untouched by decay.

Truly, how amazing are these miracles of the Christian faith. For five hundred, a thousand, a thou-

---

[120] A type of monastery usually consisting of a collection of cells or hermitages surrounding a central church, or *katholikon.—Ed.*

[121] The city is actually within the territory of Russia, although it is only a short distance from the border with Estonia and was a disputed territory between the two countries for much of the twentieth century. The monastery Fr. Daniel refers to is the Pskovo-Pechersky Dormition Monastery, or Pskov-Caves Monastery, located about 125 miles from St. Petersburg.—*Ed.*

sand five hundred years or more to have passed, and for the bodies of the saints to defy the destructive decay of the centuries. Thus they become windows through which we behold the future incorruption of Paradise under the grace of the eternal and incorrupt God.

Wondrous narratives and instances have been paraded before us. We have seen the majesty of the "imprint" of the saints, without of course having presented a great catalog of miraculous icons—a partial and indicative account. We have smelled the sweet-scented fragrances of holy relics. We have found ourselves before the mystery of incorrupt bodies.

Let all these things be considered as dew from heaven, which gives refreshment to thirsty creation. May it be that some plants that are threatened with withering will revive. And may it be that they resemble spiritual augers that will make artesian wells spring up from within us—artesian wells of faith, with abundant and pure waters that will spread life to areas made barren by unbelief—so that an ancient prophetic saying may thus be realized:

"*Be glad, O Thirsting Desert,*

Rejoice, O Desert, and blossom like a lily."

FIFTH HOMILY
(OR THE SEVEN TRUMPET CALLS)

More than nineteen centuries ago, someone who spoke about a new religion was exiled to an island in the Aegean. One Sunday he fell into ecstasy and saw stunning visions which he wrote down in a book. It was the Apostle John the Theologian, who saw and wrote Revelations, the last book of the Holy Scriptures, on Patmos.

Among other things, he also related to us the vision of the seven trumpet calls. That is, he beheld seven heavenly beings—seven angels—who held trumpets and began to blow them in succession. Each trumpet call was followed by shocking events on earth.

In this homily, we will offer the reader—as seven sacred trumpet calls—an equal number of wondrous circumstances and narratives, which can jolt the regions of unbelief with their bright supernatural majesty. They can tear down the edifices of materialism and atheism, and erect palaces of piety in their place. It is

enough, of course, for readers with good will and up-
rightness of heart to be found. Because we know that
even if souls perverted by egotism, by malice, and by
wickedness—like the Pharisees of the Gospel—behold
the resurrection of someone dead in front of them,
they are ready to contradict it. May God preserve us
from callousness of soul!

1) *The Snakes of the Panagia in Cephalonia.* Our first
trumpet call is related to an unprecedented supernatural event that is observed every August in Cephalonia.

In the south of the island, beneath the "big mountain," Mt. Ainos, in the area of Leivathos—there, where
the olive tree reigns (and from which it gets the name
Eliou[122])—we find Markopoulos. It is a small village
built at a height of three hundred meters[123] above sea
level, in the corner that looks towards the Gulf of Patras. The view is exceptional—the best balcony on
Cephalonia.

There, deep on the bank of a ravine at the Church
of the Dormition of the Theotokos, every year during

---

[122] Olive tree in Greek is 'elia' (ελιά).—*Ed.*
[123] About 984 feet.—*Ed.*

the period of the Dormition Fast,[124] the snakes of the
Panagia come out.

Ἀκίνδυνα φίδια στήν Παναγία

ΤΑ ΝΕΑ, 17·8·76

ΟΠΩΣ κάθε χρόνο στό Μαρκόπουλο τῆς Κεφαλονιᾶς ἔκαναν τήν ἐμφάνισή τους τά φίδια τῆς Παναγίας καί οἱ πιστοί δέν φοβήθηκαν νά τά πάρουν στά χέρια τους. Τά φίδια αὐτά, πού βγαίνουν κάθε χρόνο αὐτές τίς ἡμέρες, εἶναι τελείως ἀκίνδυνα, σκαρφαλώνουν στά εἰκονίσματα καί στούς πιστούς πού δέν διστάζουν νά τά παίρνουν στά χέρια τους. Ἕνα περίεργο φαινόμενο.

Harmless snakes on an icon of the Panagia and the shoulders of the faithful, as reported in a newspaper story from Markopoulos, Cephalonia. *The News (Τα Νεα)*, August 17, 1976.

From the first days of this period, specifically from
August 6th, the feast of the Transfiguration of the Savior, the famed snakes of the Panagia appear in the

---

[124] Literally, "during the period of the 'Fifteen Days' of August."—*Ed.*

church. As the days progress they increase, and on the eve of the Dormition they multiply to the point of exaggeration. While the sun is setting and the bells are ringing one after another, a very many snakes come out of their holes. You see people from Markopoulos going around the ravine with candles to gather snakes and to bring them to the church.

At vespers, when the great celebration and the unprecedented gathering of people begins, you can see snakes in every corner of the church—on the icon stands, on the stalls, and on the furniture. They circulate comfortably among the numerous pilgrims. None of them are afraid. They feel that they are all theirs. They can grab them, show them off, and lay them on top of themselves. A local couplet stresses:

"I call the snakes from Markopoulos to bite me,
but they are the Panagia's and they pet me."

The residents of Markopoulos prepare first-time pilgrims with these words: "They'll climb up onto your chest, and with the grace of the Panagia they won't harm you. You'll hold them in your hand, and they'll lick you like little cats."

An improbable and incredible phenomena—you

see some snakes wrapped around the arm of a Christian like bracelets, others that have climbed up on the icon of the Panagia, or on the Crucified One, or on the bread of the *artoklasia*.[125] During the course of the Divine Liturgy, one might climb up onto the Gospel that the priest is holding in his hands.

As representatives of the animal kingdom, they too celebrate the feast of the Mother of the Creator of all, along with the Christians. And they give the celebration an Edenic tone (in Eden, the first created humans and the animals lived in brotherhood).

When the Divine Liturgy finishes on the 15th of August, three or four photographers hold snakes in their hands and offer them to whomever wishes to be photographed with them. Some sensitive people take them with fear. Unafraid, the snakes climb up on their chests and on their necks, and the lens immortalizes the strange sight.

As August 15th takes its leave, they too depart. The Christians will expect them again on the following year "just like they expect the poppies in May," according to the expression of a Cephalonian writer. And

---

[125] The service of the Blessing of the Five Loaves.—*Ed.*

they will welcome them with sweet words: "Welcome to our beloved snakes. How have you been since last year?"

The color of these snakes is grey. In size, they are thin and relatively small. They don't exceed a meter[126] in length. When you get close to pet them on the head, you feel a velvety little skin and see two sparkling eyes.

The most impressive thing is that a small cross is formed on their broad head—something that causes a special feeling. It's something unheard of and unique; nowhere else is something similar found. Furthermore, on the edge of their thin tongue there is the sign of the cross. Some German naturalists who examined them from a zoological perspective were not able to classify them among any of the known species.

Everything related to these snakes is strange and extraordinary. Where they come from is unknown and undetermined. From the bell tower? From the cracks and crevices in the church? From the surrounding area? There is a notion that they come out of the ruins of the old church. No matter how much the people of

---

[126] A little over a yard.—*Ed.*

Markopoulos observe them to determine where they emerge, as well as where they hide after the feast, they don't notice anything. Their hiding place is unknown and mysterious.

Once a certain Christian thought of taking a snake and closing it up in a bottle! Furthermore, he placed it on his iconostasis at home. Later he discovered that the bottle was empty. As the locals tell it, in whatever place you enclose them, after forty days they disappear.

Many people who happened to have killed a snake (for instance, a cart driver who ran one over with his wagon) have seen the Panagia in their sleep, asking for its return, and decided to send silver or gold-plated wooden likenesses of snakes to her shrine. And here is something else noteworthy: When the Church of Greece adopted the new calendar in 1924, the Cephalonians were anxious to see what the snakes would do. They came out with the new calendar, something which contributed to Old-Calendarism not finding a foothold in Cephalonia. [127]

---

[127] The changeover to the new (Gregorian, or civil) calendar was accompanied by a great deal of turmoil in Greece, and many people were conflicted at the beginning about whether or not it was the right decision.

The appearance of the snakes also has a prophetic significance. It is considered a good sign for the affairs of the locality—a good year and prosperity. That is why, on the night of the 5th going into the 6th of August, the children of Markopoulos light candles and search around the bell tower with distinct anxiety to discover their appearance. The cry "the snakes have come out!" resounds, replete with great joy.

If they don't come out, it is a bad omen. In August of 1940, on the eve of the Great War, as well as in 1953 when the island was afflicted by an earthquake, they didn't come out. When unpleasant things happen to occur in Cephalonia, few of them come out. For instance in 1981, when a great deal of acrimony prevailed in the relations between the metropolitan and a portion of the flock, only two snakes appeared.

This wondrous and surprising phenomenon of the snakes of the Panagia has repeatedly occupied the press as well as the television of our country. And it has warmed up the faith of well-intentioned and upright souls.

From that year onward, the snakes came out and disappeared on the relevant dates according to the new calendar.—*Ed.*

2) *The Wondrous Well of Saint Gerasimos*. Again we'll make a stop in Cephalonia, in the area where that great saint of the sixteenth century, Gerasimos, practiced his asceticism—there where his monastery is located today. In this area, tradition says that he dug forty wells. One of these near the monastery exhibits some wondrous manifestations.

When the Saint is celebrated and his sacred body is carried around in litany, this well participates in the celebration in an impressive manner. We'll get more specific.

During the two great celebrations, on August 16th, when his repose is celebrated (for the sake of accuracy, he reposed on August 15th, but due to the feast of the One-Full-of-Grace, the feast was transferred by one day), and on October 20th when the removal of his relics is celebrated, it is established that a procession of his body occurs. When the litany reaches the well, a stop is made and prayers are offered.

At that moment, something amazing takes place. The water of the well rises up to the brim, as if it wants to behold and venerate the relics of the Saint. And the Christians, either with some container or with their hands, take water to drink and to be blessed. As soon as the day of the feast passes—more precisely, as soon as twelve o'clock midnight passes—the level of the water has fallen and has returned to the place where it was previously. In recent years, for reasons only the Lord knows, this miracle has not taken place. It seems that the Christians of olden times were more worthy of gazing upon divine signs.

Prior to 1925 another amazing thing happened. Near the well, there is a large plane tree planted by the Saint. They call it "five fingers" because of its five large branches. When the sacred relics reached there, it would bend its branches and venerate! The older people remember it and get chills recalling it.

The well of Saint Gerasimos reminds us of other similar events. It is not unusual for water associated with some sacred event or person to take care to participate in the festive commemoration of the event or of the person. It is known that an exactly similar miracle happens at the Panagia Trypiti in Aigio when it celebrates. The water of the well rises and concelebrates.

3) *Churches that Can't be Demolished.* The third trumpet call will come to us first from the north, from Sophia, the capital of Bulgaria. And a frightful trumpet call it

will be, which will proclaim that it is dangerous for the creature to rise up in insolence against the Creator.

In the central-most spot of Sophia, nestled down low in the ground, there was a beautiful and ancient little church of Saint Petka; that is, of Saint Paraskevi (in Bulgarian, the sixth day of the week is called 'Petak')[128]—not the familiar virgin-martyr, but a saint of the same name who is particularly honored there, and whose relics are found in Romania today. Impressive and terrific events are associated with this church, which made the "powerful" of the earth submit their will to some other invincible will and power.

Around 1963, the relevant authorities decided to widen the main road. This meant that the Christian monument had to be razed to the ground. Thus they would also be rid of an undesirable edifice.[129] The demolition crew got ready. A bulldozer would play the first role. Within a few minutes, it would turn it into a pile ruins. That was how they had reckoned things, but matters came out upside down for them. Another song was playing, and not the one that they wanted.

---

[128] In Greek, the sixth day of the week (Friday) is called 'Paraskevi', which means 'preparation' (i.e. for the Sabbath); hence the parallel.—*Ed.*
[129] At the time, Bulgaria, like most other Eastern European countries, was an atheistic Communist state.—*Ed.*

While they were starting up the bulldozer and pointing it towards the Church, it would constantly break down. They would fix it, but it would break again. It was impossible for them to get near the church. And as if that were not enough, as soon as the worker who was trying to tear it down in a rage arrived home, he found one of his family members dead!

In the meantime, the person responsible for this undertaking was informed that the workers had not managed to do anything. He also found out the details.

Church of St. Petka in Sophia, Bulgaria, which resisted demolition.

It all seemed nonsensical to him, and, enraged, he said to them: "You're not worth anything. You're just for fairy tales. Tomorrow I'll go and tear it down myself!"

But the unfortunate man was left with only his boastful words. As soon as he climbed up on the machine in a rage and put it in gear towards the church, it too broke down; and—the most shocking thing of all—he himself also met a sudden death! You can imagine what grief and also what terror followed. Nothing else remained but to rescind the order to raze it. And in order to beautify the area, they built something like underground shops and a plaza around the church, as shown in the previous photograph.

It became known throughout all of Sophia that Saint Petka, or rather He whom the Saint worshipped, had incalculable power which, if He started to show it at some point, would seize everyone with panic.

There are a large number of supernatural events of this kind. There are also other churches, which had some particular significance and history within Christianity, and which, as soon as they faced demolition, neutralized it in a way that caused amazement. This has also happened to churches that did not have any particular outstanding value, except however that by repulsing the enemy, they strengthened the faith of many people.

Around 1968, the cemetery church of Saint George in Phragoleika (a small village in Aetolia, after Kleisoura and before Agrinio) forced the Antirrio-Arta-Ioannina highway into a nasty detour. The same supernatural events took place. Moreover, they left the machine that broke down as it set out to tear down the church broken there, and only once the entire project was finished did they dare to approach it and fix it.

Two other churches in the area of Skaramaga in Elefsina belong to the same category. One of these, the Dormition of the Theotokos, at the edge of the shipyards of the shipowner Niarchos,[130] broke some enormous demolition equipment on them when they went to tear it down in order to continue building the high wall. They finally decided to make a small curve and to leave it untouched, "outside the walls." They could have enclosed it inside, because the space allowed it,

---

[130] Stavros Spyros Niarchos (1909-1996) was a Greek shipping tycoon and multi-billionaire, who built some of the first and biggest oil super-tankers in the early 1950s.—*Ed.*

Church of St. George in Phragouleika.

but the fright they got made them pull back inside!

The other one, by the name of the Transfiguration, is near Lake Koumoundourou. Around 1963 they built an asphalt road there, towards Upper Liosia. Thus, on the official road along the sea shore, where from Athens it continued on towards Elefsina, a branch road would be opened to the right in the direction we mentioned.

As they had drawn the plan, the chapel gave them trouble, and the order was given for them to tear it down. (Who knows what god the one who gave such orders worshipped?) And here the same wondrous things resulted. The blade of the excavator broke twice, whereupon they realized that they had to submit to a higher will. Thus the curve was made a little further down, and the little church with its beautiful dome continues to send its blessing and its greetings to all the passersby on the much-frequented road next to it.

Similar stories are encountered in the area of Athens, as well. A Byzantine chapel that exists at a low level near the Cephissos River, St. Nicholas "the Sunken"—an ancient catacomb at the entrance of the station for long-distance buses to the Peloponnese, very beautiful and ancient—humbled the haughty eyebrows of certain impious people. It first broke a small bulldozer and following that a larger one. They were terrified and they left it in its place.

At Saint John in Neos Kosmos,[131] behind the altar of this majestic church and right next to Vouliagmenis

---

[131] This neighborhood, literally meaning "New World," is in south-central Athens.—*Ed.*

Avenue, there exists the small old Saint John's. When the large one was built, they said that, since it was superfluous, they should tear it down. But the same things happened here, too. The bulldozers broke down, and so they left it. We should note that the holiest priest of old Athens, Papa-Nicholas Planas[132] served in this little church.

All of these cases are amazing and invigorating for faith, and at the same time they are symbolic as well. They show the indestructible power of the Church of Christ. "The gates of Hades shall not prevail against it."[133]

4) *Strange Energies of the Possessed.* The fourth trumpet call will resemble water coming from an unclean spring, from the demons. It is not in a Christian's interest to be occupied with demonic phenomena. He has the Light and he doesn't need the darkness. To captives of materialism however, demonic phenomena show that a spiritual world exists—spirits, demons, angels—as Christianity proclaims. Thus the tree of unbelief is struck and the flower of faith sprouts anew.

---

[132] St. Nicholas Planas (1932✝) was canonized as a saint by the Ecumenical Patriarch in 1992, after the publication of Fr. Daniel's book.—*Ed.*
[133] Mt 16:18—*Ed.*

There is even frequent talk in the Gospels about persons possessed by unclean spirits. However, we will occupy ourselves with contemporary cases. These persons are easily found during holidays at large pilgrimage sites. Moreover, during the Divine Liturgy, when the Holy Gifts pass by, they emit terrible cries that make the congregation freeze from surprise and fright.

The first time I had such an impressive experience was quite a few years ago in the Peloponnese, in the prefecture of Elias. There at a large pilgrimage site, at the Sacred Monastery of St. Athanasios (Karakouzi) on the day of the celebration, January 18th, a possessed woman performed signs and terrors. At the time of the Divine Liturgy, when they were trying to take her to commune, she turned the place upside down with shouts and curses. As soon as the priests took the cross from the holy altar and crossed her, she cried out heartrendingly: "The blood of Christ burned me!" When she finally communed, she calmed down completely and her enraged face took on an angelic grace.

They take many possessed people to Cephalonia for the celebration of Saint Gerasimos, who has a special charisma "against demons." Furthermore, when his holy relics pass next to them, they howl as if divine flames were scourging them: "You burned us, Burner!"

"Burner!" That's what they call the Saint—and the pilgrimage sites "furnaces!" They like to use nicknames for sacred persons. A possessed woman from Piraeus, Catherine Krakari—quite a few decades have gone by now—with a terrible demon, when they took her to all-night vigils in various churches, would shout: "Everyone in here is blah-blah-blah-ing about the One-Nailed-to-the-Wood!" That's how she called Christ. "Me," it (the demon) said to Krakari, "Fingernails will get me out of you. No one else will be able to." It meant Saint Nectarios. This was explained when, on his first exhumation, the Saint was found incorrupt and with his fingernails having grown. She really was healed by Saint Nectarios and, as the nun Parthenia, she spent the rest of her life at his monastery in Aegina.

A possessed woman from Patras, named Maria Kapsalis, as soon as she ends up in a Divine Liturgy, becomes enraged. Many times she shouts: "Why, the priest is slaughtering Christ on the holy altar! Boy, we have one Dawn-bearer and we honor him, and you have one Christ and you slaughter Him!" (Satan is called Dawn-bearer.)[134] Likewise, moments come when she makes like a frog. At other times she speaks foreign languages. Once she said that, "We devils rejoice three times a year: in the summer, with the beachgoing; on New Year's night, with the card-playing; and at Mardi Gras with the carnivals."

Phenomena of group possession are even observed once in a while, such as, for example, the famous "Ceramia Events" in Crete, south of Chania. There, around the end of the eighteenth century, a great sacrilege occurred at the Monastery of the Holy Trinity, northeast of Chania. An excommunication followed—they were accustomed to something like that during the time of Turkish rule—both for whomever committed it and for whomever knew about it and did not bear witness.

The result was dreadful. All of the villages in the Ceramia area (Papadiana, Loulos, Panagia, Aletrouvari, Cambos, etc.) were plagued by the malice of the demons. Quarrels, fights, the dissolution of families, misfortunes, intimidations, deaths. In the afternoons,

---

[134] The more familiar English equivalent is Lucifer, which in Latin means 'Light-bearer', however in this particular context we have chosen to use a literal translation of the Greek term, in order for Fr. Daniel's parenthetic explanation to make more sense.—*Ed.*

people were afraid to pass by ravines with plane trees. And the demonic possession of many people; during a certain period, there were forty-two possessed people. Unbelievable things happened.

Sometimes the demons would take possessed people out of their beds at night and take them to the most inaccessible caves of Samaria. They would bring them back, while one of their shoes might remain in the cave, so that the disbelievers would find it later on and believe. The teacher, C. Kostourakis, writes about one possessed woman of the area that: "There did not remain one cave large or small, or lake or river, or far away corner where it did not take her. They did not leave a ravine or dry well, canyon or cliff, or fathomless pit upon the earth where they did not take her up and down."[135]

Other times they would hang them at night from wild pear trees and leave them there until the morning hours! Or at other times the possessed people, when they took them to the Divine Liturgy, would sing the most beautiful Cretan songs in order to hinder the priests. They would also say things which resembled

[135] Constantine A. Kostourakis, *The Ceramia Events* (*Τα Κεραμιανα*), Chania, 1977, p. 42.

oracles or revelations. Thus the phrase came about: "the preachers said this."

Ninety percent of this whole story came to an end on October 3, 1936, with the lifting of the excommunication—the "unexcommunication"—which the Metropolitan of Chania, Agathangelos, performed on the spot. A certain elderly man who happened to be present at the service, remembers—and mentioned it to me—that the demons hurled threats against the bishop: "Cuckold priest, we won't let you unexcommunicate them!"

Throughout all of Crete, the phrase "the devils of Ceramia" has been established as a proverb. A couplet even tells them:

> *"Demons appeared in a whole lot of little trunks,*
> *They sprinkled little poisons on them all by okes."*[136]

And in Mournies of Chania, behind the church of the Archangel Michael, there is the tomb of a possessed woman who had the biggest demonic catalepsy. The inscription reads:

---

[136] There is some clever wordplay here, since the Greek word for 'trunks' (as in tree trunks) also means 'bodies', and the Greek word for 'little poisons' also refers to the insecticides farmers use on their trees. An *oke* is a local unit of measurement, weighing a little less than three pounds.—*Ed.*

"HERE LIES OLGA KANTILIERAKIS, FOR 16 YEARS SEIZED BY THE DEMON AND LED INTO THE WILDERNESS, MIRACULOUSLY HEALED DURING THE UNEXCOMMUNICATION OF 10-3-1936.... REPOSED IN THE LORD ON 4-29-1969 AT THE AGE OF 59 YEARS."

Phenomena of group possession also appeared at the beginning of the 1980s in Xiromeros of Aetolia-Acarnania, in the village of Babini. Whereas in Ceramia the cause was sacrilege, here it was blasphemy. "In our village, they blaspheme mercilessly," a certain man from Babini admitted. The epicenter of the phenomena was a family from the village, and most especially one of its members, Stathis, a lanky boy of thirteen. The child had been oppressed very much, and moreover by his grandmother, and ended up in a spiritual derangement, whereupon an evil spirit—and furthermore, one of the strongest—found suitable circumstances to take control of him.

How could anyone dare to approach the house where Stathis lived? He would be risking his life. But the evil was also poured out onto the whole village. The villagers cried out: "We are lost! Our village has become haunted!"

Here is a sad list of the demonic afflictions: They would tie their horses or their animals somewhere, and strangely they would find them untied. They would go to the storage shed and see the tap of the wine or oil casks opened. A strong wind would blow and take the roofs of the houses. Terrible rainstorms would break out and destroy the tobacco crop.

They would go to sleep, and when they woke up they would feel salt on their heads. Whoever entered Stathis' house could see a sandal take flight, or an icon coming at his head, or rounded rocks as from a river—which indicated that they were coming loose from the wall—falling next to him!

Observe now an excerpt from a letter from the people of Babini to the state authorities:

"Beside our unimaginable misfortune due to the last storm, terror has also been added lately. Our village has become haunted. Ghosts appear who throw rocks and icons. We have literally lost it. We don't know which we should talk about first: our poverty, the haunting, or our complete abandonment by the State? ... Five hundred people are living in terror. The storm did not leave any-thing standing. The roofs of the houses have almost completely come off. The tobacco, our only income, has

been destroyed by the rain.... (And the signature) The
Council of the Unfortunate Residents of the Community
of Babini, Xiromeros, Aetolia-Acarnania"[137]

Hellenic Television even dealt with this issue
repeatedly on the show *Reporters.*

The evil finally ended when an elderly hieromonk
who practiced asceticism in the region of Attica went
to Babini in October of 1983, on the eve of the feast of
Saint Demetrios. He found Stathis in the courtyard of
the church, crossed him, read prayers over him, gave
him the appropriate admonitions, and freed him from
the demonic possession. It is worth underlining that
while Stathis knelt and the elder held the cross above
his head, a mighty power threatened to yank the cross
far away out of the priest-monk's hands.

His parents, to whom the elder gave the necessary
counsels, did not know how to thank him—how to express their limitless gratitude. They wanted to offer
him many gifts, such as, for instance, the choicest
cheese from their sheepfold; but the only thing he
would accept was a little rustic bread.

This does not concern illusions or fairytales, but

---

[137] As reported in *The Meridian*, November 1, 1982.

very vivid realities about which research, publications, and television programs speak. Regarding the events of Ceramia, we refer to a specific literary work, *The Ceramia Events*,[138] by Constantine Kostourakis, a teacher.

Many times people who are possessed exhibit two astonishing phenomena during their demonic crisis. The first one is that they reveal the sins of various persons—they "air their dirty laundry." And the second is that they speak foreign languages. It may be, for instance, that they speak Swedish to a foreigner from Sweden, and Dutch to one from Holland! A certain possessed person who went from Greece to Jerusalem spoke to the tourists in their own language and revealed their sins to them. Let it be noted that after the passage of the demonic crisis, the person has no idea of the foreign languages that he spoke before.

These are a few things about the possessed. Their message is that the world does not consist only of matter and of sensory things. There are also supersensory things—the immaterial and the spiritual—those things which unbelief wants to write off.

---

[138] Op. cit. (see note 131).

5) _The Blood of the Hieromartyr Januarius._ The fifth trumpet call will come to us from southern Italy, a land that was once _Magna Graecia_,[139] and it will present us with an exceedingly wondrous event related to an ancient hero of Christianity, Saint Januarius, or "San Gennaro" as the Italians call him.

The aforementioned saint—the popular, wonder-working patron saint of Naples and protector of Campania—lived more than seventeen centuries ago. He was a shepherd over the sheep of Christ—that is to say, a bishop in the area of Benevento (southern Italy). On September 19, 305 A.D., his Christian faith cost him a martyr's death by beheading. The terrible persecution of Diocletian[140] had broken out at that time.

The Christians gathered a quantity of his blood, which is preserved today in two small vials in a glass case in his large church in Naples. It is a black-reddish spongelike mass; but on his feast, on September 19th, an unprecedented miracle happens. The thickened and dried blood liquefies—something which spreads

---

[139] _Magna Graecia_, or 'Great Greece', was comprised of the ancient Greek colonies along the southern coastal areas of Italy, including Sicily, dating back to the 8th century B.C.—_Ed._

[140] Diocletian, who reigned from 284 to 305 B.C., was the 51st Roman emperor. The persecution he started against the Christians was the last and arguably the most severe in the history of the Roman Empire.—_Ed._

The Holy Hieromartyr Januarius, Bishop of Benevento.

the greatest joy among the numerous multitudes of believers who flood the church. On that day, thousands of people from all over Italy are found there—clergymen, lay people, rulers and authorities, police, reporters, television cameras, and even many non-believers and people who are curious.

The amazing liquefaction begins from one spot—sometimes from the middle, and other times from the edge—and extends to the whole mass. Likewise, it can happen earlier or later—usually a half hour or an hour from when the Mass begins. The liquefied blood remains in this condition for quite a few hours, and sometimes even for quite a few days—even as many as eight days. Its return to solidification is accomplished in stages: from liquid to semiliquid to dough-like to solid.

Case holding two small vials of the dried blood of Saint Januarius.

The miracle also occurs on May 31st, when the translation of the Saint's relics takes place. If it does not happen in some year, such as in 1944 for instance, it is considered a bad sign. A necessary condition for the liquefaction is for the Saint's icon to be nearby.

Sometimes the miracle takes on another form. Red

bubbles appear in the liquefied matter. Then they say that "the Saint's blood is boiling." And there is another

First close-up photograph of the blood of St. Januarius as it was beginning to liquefy, taken by Venetian photographer Dino Jarach and published in the weekly newspaper *La Domenica del Corriere* on October 2, 1975.

amazing thing: In Pozzuoli, a picturesque city on the Gulf of Naples (in ancient times it was a Greek colony belonging to Kymi), the marble on which they beheaded him is preserved at the Church of San Gennaro. It is painted a color like red and like rust. When the liquefaction takes place in Naples, then, this marble slab takes on an intense bloody color. It appears bloodied, drenched with sublimated blood.

In relation to the liquefaction of the blood of Saint Januarius, human science cannot say anything. What can it say? A dead mass—a solid substance—suddenly comes alive and changes color, mass, weight and properties, only to return again to its former state. And this is repeated throughout the centuries. All the biological facts are invalidated. No scientific explanation can shed light on the phenomenon.

The only interpretation is faith in the omnipotence of Christ, who has authority over all natural laws. Furthermore, it is he for whom the Saint shed his blood. Indeed, in killing the bishop of Benevento and the other Christians, his executioners even thought that they were wounding the Christian Church. But the complete opposite happened; they offered it the greatest benefaction. They adorned it with heroes and martyrs and miracles.

Let's note that when Saint Januarius was martyred in 305 A.D., he belonged to the one, unified Church of Christ.

6) *Strange Phenomena at the Beach on Chios*. Whoever finds himself at a certain seashore on Chios—in the northwestern section of the island, west of Volissos, the ancient homeland of Homer—on July 22nd will be astonished by the sea of people. He would think that all of Chios has gathered there.

What in the world is happening? Why this flood of people? The reason is religious. There, on a small rock upon which they have set up a cross, is the holy spring of the Virgin-Martyr Markella of Chios.

On this spot about four centuries ago, this saint— full of every bodily and spiritual grace—met a martyr's death at the age of eighteen. And by whose hand, do you think? By that of her own father—a vicious type, vulgar and perverse. Because she did not consent to his shameful and immoral suggestions, he chased her down and killed her in this location.

He could not touch her purity, however. Something marvelous happened, like that which happened with the First-Martyr Thecla. A large rock at the edge of the sea opened and received her body, up to her chest. As if rabid, he took a knife and cut off her arms, her breasts and her head, which he threw in a rage— some pieces towards the mountain and others towards the sea. His bestial passions reduced him to a daughter killer.

The monastery of Saint Markella on Chios, Greece.

The rock which received the martyr's undefiled body is found just barely inside the sea. If it happens to get stormy, it covers it. It issues water which is considered blessed. This is the holy spring of Saint Markella. It is brackish and warm, and naturally it gets mixed in with and dissolves inside the sea water. Further up, at a distance of about one kilometer, lies her monastery.

A miraculous icon of hers is kept there, as well.

We said that on July 22nd, on her feast day that is, a great gathering of people is observed, who go moreover from the day before because they have to attend the all-night vigil; and they fast, in order to drink from the holy spring. Of course, among such a multitude there are also some distrusting, uninvolved or even unbelieving people who come out of curiosity. A certain supernatural event that is expected to take place at the site of the Saint's martyrdom also attracts them.

That is, as soon as the Divine Liturgy finishes at the monastery, they all go down to the seashore, to the holy spring. And just as the priest begins the supplication service of the Saint—"To the prizewinner let us the faithful now run, the sick and the healthy and fall down before..."—a one-of-a-kind miracle is made manifest. The holy water begins to boil, as if you had placed a powerful fire beneath it.

The surface fills with steam and bubbles. The eyes of everyone are fixed there. As warm as the faith of the virgin-martyr was, the water also becomes as warm. Whoever puts his hand in it understands it better—a strange and supernatural boiling. The faithful are moved. The unbelievers are perplexed.

The Holy Virgin-Martyr Markella of Chios.

This miracle does not happen only on the Saint's feast day, but every time the supplication service is performed. As soon as the sacred service is completed, the boiling subsides, the steam vanishes and the former condition returns.

If this strange boiling does not take place on some occasion, it means that one of the people present is not clean. As soon as this person departs, the miracle takes place. When a very virtuous priest happens to perform the supplication service, the boiling becomes more intense and powerful steam is emitted from the opening of the rock from which the holy water issues.

And there is another supernatural sign. While the pebbles, the stones, and the cliffs throughout the area have a black coloring, there where the wounded saint walked and was slaughtered, and where her blood was splattered, the color is reddish. An older text speaks of "pebbles full of congealed blood." Despite the fact that the sea has been lapping at them for centuries now, the crimson coloration is preserved intensely and impressively. It is to remind us of the contest of the brave Markella.

At the holy spring, as well as at the monastery, a thousand and one miracles and healings of suffering people are performed. This is witnessed by the innumerable dedications which literally choke the icon of the saint. In 1965, blood ran from a spot on the neck of this miraculous icon that is at the monastery, and a little girl shouted: "Mom, look! Blood!" It was one miracle after another—because, until then, the little girl had been mute!

Pilgrims visit the holy spring of Saint Markella.

Many times, water from the holy spring that is kept in a bottle becomes like blood, or drops of blood are present at the bottom. But also on the surface of the sea at the holy spring—there, where her father threw her head—at certain times during the supplication service or at some other time, red foam appears. "In former times," the locals comment, "when people were purer, it appeared often."

Now that we are talking about these things, the thought occurs that, just as in our days wondrous appearances of the blood of martyrs (of Saint Markella or Saint Januarius) are realized that anyone can discern, it also happened exactly that way in olden times, just like the *Synaxaria* of the martyrs report to us. Today's reality corroborates the reality of yesterday.

Related to this, we'll mention an amazing instance involving the relics of the Great-Martyr Euphemia. She was martyred in the third century A.D. in Chalcedon. Her final martyrdom was to be thrown into the city's stadium as food for hungry bears.

Every year at her feast, some drops of blood would spill out of her silver-adorned tomb. The bishop of the city would gather them. The exceptional phenomenon they exhibited was that they gave off an ineffably sweet fragrance. And every year the Christians ran to see and to smell the droplets.

One thing brings to mind another; the tomb of the Virgin-Martyr Euphemia brings us to the tomb of the Forerunner.

In Damascus, Syria, there is a majestic monastery church of Saint John the Forerunner, built by Justinian.[141] From the time when the Arabs conquered the area (in the 8th century A.D.), it was changed into a Muslim temple. Nevertheless, in one part of the colossal church there is a wonderful, artistic and rather large mausoleum. It is the tomb of the precious head of the Baptist. Whether they wanted to or not, the Arabs were forced to preserve it, and furthermore to cover it with a very luxurious canopy and to adorn it with gold.

After the fourth finding of the head of Saint John, the recovered relic was kept by Justinian as a treasure in a beautiful casket. When the Muslims converted the church into a mosque, they also tampered with the tomb. But they were terrified because, with the first blows of the pickaxe, warm blood started coming out of it and continued running for several days and nights. It would not stop.

Panicked, the Arabs asked the Christian patriarch to pray. He, along with all of the sacred clergy of Damascus, performed three days of litanies around the

---

[141] Justinian I, also known as 'Justinian the Great', was Byzantine (Roman) emperor from 527 to 565 A.D. Among his many splendid accomplishments were the restoration of large parts of the western Roman Empire, the recodification of Roman law, and the building of numerous churches (including the magnificent Hagia Sophia) and other Christian and civil monuments.—*Ed.*

tomb, whereupon the blood stopped on the third day. Special writing on top of the monument, with Arabic letters in gold, relates this stunning event. To this day the Muslim world greatly respects the tomb of the Forerunner, and at the same time fears it. They don't dare come near it!

Let's return, however, to the holy spring of the Virgin-Martyr Markella. It is very common for mothers to bring their sick children there to wash them—and the miracle is not long in happening. It has been characterized as the "spring of miracles."

Years ago (in 1966), a junior-high-school girl was suffering from a dermatological disease. Having come with her family from the Congo in Africa to the city of Chios (to Saint John Atsikis), she felt the bad effect on her from the change in climate. She broke out in pimples that no salve or therapy could heal. She made up her mind and went to the holy spring, and that was it. She was delivered forever from her annoying disease.

Cures have even occurred with the blood-colored pebbles. "Many people put the pebbles in jars and they have them for the cure of every illness."[142] Certainly,

---

[142] Sophronius Eustratiados, *Book of Saints of the Orthodox Church.* Athens: Apostolic Ministry of the Church of Greece. 1950.

whoever is deemed worthy and arrives there as a pilgrim will feel these things vividly. And the degrees on their thermometer of faith will definitely rise.

7) *The Pilgrimage of Saint Theodora of Vasta.* In the prefecture of Arcadia, on the border of Messenia, on the outskirts of Megalopolis, is the village Vasta. One of its chapels honors the name of the local Saint Theodora, the Venerable Virgin-Martyr, who is celebrated on September 11th. This little church is unique in all the world. Such a chapel as this has never existed before, nor shall it ever again. It is entirely a miracle that shatters unbelief.

In a miraculous and inexplicable way, seventeen trees—oaks and maples, each one of which exceeds ten meters[143]—have grown on top of it. Despite all of their weight, and despite all the blowing of the wind, they stand there completely upright on a roof which was made ten centuries ago. What is worthy of curiosity is the fact that no roots can be distinguished on the inside of the roof.

A pious pilgrim notes: "How did so many trees sprout, grow, and continue to be maintained on top of

---

[143] About 33 feet.—*Ed.*

a ten-century-old roof? How can there be so much weight up there? How is it that when strong winds blow, whose powers are multiplied, it doesn't collapse in a heap, but stands proudly like a bouquet of flowers? As you are arriving and you see it from afar, your

The Holy Martyr Theodora of Vasta.

The chapel of St. Theodora, with its 17 trees.

lips will stammer, "Great art Thou, O Lord, and wondrous are Thy works...."

And beneath the little church, water runs. A sparkling spring that gushes miraculously from the rocky ground. Blessed water which remains free from putrefaction, like holy water.

The church, the trees, and the spring are on the spot where Saint Theodora was unjustly slaughtered, the victim of a very grave slander. And they remind one of one of the Saint's last beseeching phrases before her martyrdom: "My God and my Lord, may my body become a church, may my blood become a river, and my hair trees!"

There is a cinematographic film about the Saint's life and her one-of-a-kind shrine by the Orthodox "Apostle Barnabas" Institute. A festive liturgical gathering takes place every Easter Tuesday and on August 16th at this sacred place.

✤ ✤ ✤

As in olden times the important trumpet players raised the enthusiasm of the warriors and animated them, thus in the same way these seven trumpet calls that we have been worthy of hearing raise up the level of faith. As in the time of Jesus of Navi,[144] they bring down the walls of the Jericho that is called unbelief.

They further reinforce and raise up the strength of spiritual vision. Thus we discover unknown paths that lead us to exceptional places. Thus we find out about

---

[144] To readers of most English-language translations of the Bible, this figure is better known as Joshua of Nun.—*Ed.*

fruitful trees with fruits that we taste for the first time in our lives. Thus, from poor people wearing rags, we become rich with a wealth that no decay or threat can destroy. Wealthy magnates! How beautifully that most wise ascetic, Isaac the Syrian, put it: "There is not enough room in heaven or on earth for the treasures of faith!"

Whoever is barren of faith becomes impoverished on all levels of life. His existence is rendered faint of heart and shriveled. His horizons become suffocatingly narrow. His perspectives are unimaginably limited. The oak tree is forced to develop in a flowerpot!

Without reference to, and rearing in, the eternal Principal, whatever an unbeliever may think or say or do ends up, in the final analysis, "empty walnuts and skins full of air," according to the words of Makrygiannis. May he who "is able to do all things" take pity on our poverty and deliver us from the wretchedness of unbelief, enriching us with the gold and pearls of faith, with its sacred and inestimable treasures for which "there is not enough room in heaven or on earth."

Poetic Addendum

Strengthening

My friend,
  if the shrew of unbelief gnashes her teeth at you,
  do not be frightened, neither cower.
Take up weapons and strike her.
Send the snakes from Markopoulos to bite her—
  the only time they ever bite.
Prick her with the bush of Sinai also.
And stone her with onions from Oxylithos.
If with stubbornness she does resist,
  do not forget the Archangel at Mandamados'
  grim face.
Use even the sword of the Panormitis,
  which flashes like lightning, "the one of great
  grace," and first in maritime glory.

Is the all-joyous Pascha close to sinking in you?
Run to smell the little lilies of the Panagia,
  wherever it is convenient for you—
  in Cephalonia, in Leipsi, in Andros…

In their buds, a mystical script,

   "I await the resurrection of the dead...."

I see that you have a mania for tourism.

Well, then fly

   to Saint Petka in Sophia

   or to the caves of Kiev—

   I say, how many incorrupt relics are there!—

   a bright preview of some future

   unshakable life.

Visit Naples also,

   just make it at the feast of San Gennaro,

   at the time of the great shout of joy.

"The dry tree is made to flourish"—

   thus wrote Ezekiel,

   the seer of the cherubic chariot.

Going east, make a stop in Palestine.

The catfish of the Jordan will welcome you,

   showing you a certain dove.

You will also see the relics of an ascetic, Savvas,

   incorrupt and fragrant for a thousand five hundred

   years now!

On the morning of the sixth of August,

Don't forget the cloud of Tabor;

It will remind you of some other Cloud.
Gaze also upon that split column
   which the light rent asunder.
The main thing: Allow your eyes,
   on Holy Saturday in the great church
   amidst shouts and claps,
   to be caressed by the Holy Light,
   not made by hands, living, flying,
   bluish in the beginning,
   and the three first minutes not burning!

If you are sleeping in the boat of poverty
   and your wings cannot bear distant flights,
   ask others about these unheard of things.
Nevertheless, see "with your own eyes"
   how your neighbor makes *prosphora* with a flower
   from the cross.
   Yes, without leavening, without the action of
   bacteria!
Also ask your parish priest for
   a bottle of holy water.
   Do the experiment with that ...

Examine furthermore,
   why Thessalonica rose up on October 26th—

were the other three-hundred sixty something days
all lost?—
and how Mytilini was delivered on November 8ᵗʰ.
Investigate a few other things as well—
what happened at Philiatra with Kondau,
at Orchomenos with Hoffmann,
and at Arachova with Vlachower...
Certainly, the Germans were reconciled with the
saints!

I would mention many other things to you too,
all strengthening,
all "arrows of the Mighty One"
and rounded rocks "from the brook,"
which throw down in a heap
that heartless giant of the Philistines.

But, so that you know it, the highest thing of all is
the "Increase our faith."[145]
You are a violin, your good will is the bow,
and the melody:
"Lord, increase our faith."

---

[145] Lk 17:5—*Ed.*

<u>FAITH</u> (by G. Drosini)

Do you not have faith, when your stalks
   to bear wheat you await,
and when from the fruitless tree you grafted,
   a fruitful shoot you anticipate?

   Faith you have, when from barren ground
     and from lightning-burned sticks
     you expect the freshest fruits
     and leaves green and thick.

Do you not have faith, when going
   along a mountain road, you seek
to arrive at the ethereal heights
   of some dumbfounding peak?

   Faith you have, when bound in chains
     deep in the midst of the abyss,
     you expect your body to fly free
     up to heavenly bliss!

Do you not have faith, when in the evening
   you wait for the stars out to peek,
and with the rooster's crowing
   the dawn to shine, smiling rose-cheeked?

Faith you have, when—however irrational and
    deceiving your mind, know it though it may—
    you await the sun at midnight
    and the starlight at midday!

Do you not have faith, when believing,
    you ask for judgment and for knowledge?
Do you not have faith, when you have based
    your faith on logic?

  Faith you have, when your every dream
    you light as a votive on her altar,
    and if some vow of yours is impossible,
    you wait for the miracle to occur!

<u>HOLY FAITH</u>... (by K. Palamas)

Holy faith of my fathers come to me
and fill up my heart for me,
speak sweetly and laugh inside of me
like children full of glee.

    And in the Jordan wash me
    from my faults, and just for once
    do also to me
    what the mystical Dove does!

Embolden my soul and also teach me
to be willing, to be able,
and cast away from my opinions every
cowardly, chilling gale.

    Every wisdom and knowledge of this world
    which brings about dizziness great,
    instead of throwing pure oil on my fire,
    make my soul to hate!

Of unbelief—alas!—take the caterpillar out of me,
And of suspicion the nails,
and let not glitter many-headed before me,
either Truth or Beauty.

And make my mind like the villager's
industrious hand,
always digging, always sowing
something in his paternal land.

Light in me that uncontainable flame
that moves everything forward,
And on the earth crown me a victor
over ruin and war!

<u>VESPERS</u> (by L. Porphyra)

Mute souls, aggrieved! And in the evening
they wait for our Christ, from afar,
who knows, from how far away. And he is coming
in the haze of the autumn air.

> With the holy light his misty-lighted crown,
> with his divinely lowered eyes—
> Alone. And the dry leaves for him spread around
> golden carpets on the deserted byways.

The sparrows of the field and those in flight,
which return flocking to their homes,
as soon as they see him bow with delight,
low they fly and him do they welcome.

> The darkness thinly woven, half transparent,
> just enough to cover him in its soot,
> and the naked branches lift up like hands
> and pray at his immaterial route.

Silently they pray...And he comes
and bends down to the souls awaiting him,
gently...compassionately. And the semantron,[146]
it too compassionate, slowly and softly chimes...

---

[146] For an explanation of the term 'semantron' see note 18 (p. 32).—*Ed.*

About the Translators

Father Nicholas Palis is a graduate of Hellenic College and of the Theological School of the Aristotelian School of Theology at the University of Thessaloniki. He has served as a priest at the Annunciation Greek Orthodox Church in Lancaster, PA, and at the Dormition of the Theotokos Greek Orthodox Church in Aliquippa, PA. He currently serves as the Oeconomus, Dean, and presiding priest of the Saint Nicholas Greek Orthodox Cathedral in Bethlehem, Pennsylvania.

While studying in Greece prior to his ordination, Fr. Nicholas had the blessing of meeting a number of holy elders, such as Elder Paisios, Archimandrite Sophrony of Essex, Fr. Philotheos Zervakos, and the recently glorified Saint Porphyrios, to name a few. Because of his great respect for such holy people, he has translated from Greek to English many books, pamphlets, bulletins and magazine articles, several of which have been published in the U.S. and abroad.

As a strong believer in the importance of Orthodox

education for children, Fr. Nicholas has served on the boards of several Orthodox schools, including the Three Hierarchs Eastern Orthodox School in Pittsburgh, PA, the All Saints Eastern Orthodox School in the Poconos region of Pennsylvania, and St. Nicholas Academy in Bethlehem, PA.

Married since 1987, he and his Presvytera, Irene, have five children and two grandchildren.

✦ ✦ ✦

Lawrence Damian Robinson is a graduate of Harvard University and of the Johns Hopkins University's School of Advanced International Studies. He worked for many years in the financial services industry, has traveled extensively around the world, and has lived in several countries.

Baptized into the holy Orthodox Christian faith in 1996 in Oxford, England, Damian has since translated and edited a number of Orthodox Christian books from Greek to English. Among these are a number of historical fiction novels for Orthodox teens and young adults, on which he collaborated with his wife.

He currently lives in Greece with his wife, Efrosyni, and their son, Lucas.

INDEX

ALSO FROM EPIGNOSIS PUBLISHING

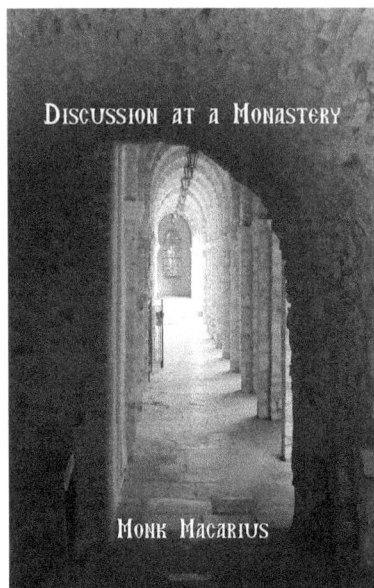

"You shall be perfect, even as your Father Who is in the heavens is perfect." (Mt 5:48) These words of our Lord and Savior Jesus Christ represent one of the most daunting of the commandments he has given his followers. But how are we to accomplish such a lofty task, living in a world full of turmoil, distractions, and challenges to our spiritual progress?

In simple but powerful language, *Discussion at a Monastery* addresses questions about the meaning of Orthodox Christian monasticism, and of the spiritual life in general, based on the real-life experiences of a contemporary Greek Orthodox monk and his fellow spiritual laborers.

Far from being suited only to monastics, however, this profound little book contains deep spiritual insights that will illumine the souls of all readers. At the same time, it will challenge anyone who is interested in developing a clearer understanding of the nature of the spiritual life—which is fundamentally a life of prayer—to first develop a clearer understanding of his or her own inner nature.

ISBN: 978 0 615986739. Available at www.epignosispublishing.com and in print and e-book format at Amazon.com. Volume discounts available for parish bookstores and distributors ordering 10 or more copies. Address all inquiries to: publisher@epignosispublishing.com.

www.ingramcontent.com/pod-product-compliance
Lightning Source LLC
LaVergne TN
LVHW051046080426
835508LV00019B/1732